PSYCHOLOGICAL TIGHT SPACES:

ONE BLACK FEMINIST SCHOLAR'S
JOURNEY INTO ACADEMIA

Shawn Arango Ricks

Produced and Distributed By:

Library Partners Press

ZSR Library

Wake Forest University

1834 Wake Forest Road

Winston-Salem, North Carolina 27106

library partners press

a digital publishing imprint

www.librarypartnerspress.org

To my husband,

Darrell Ricks,

whose love, patience, and support

made this project possible.

To my children,

Imani, Nia, and Nathan,

my faith, purpose, and gifts from God.

CONTENTS

PROLOGUE

When I dare to be powerful,
to use my strength in the service of my vision,
then it becomes less and less important
whether I am afraid
—Audre Lorde

My mother and grandmother valued education. Although limited in their knowledge and exposure to the formal system of education, they believed that if I or any Black child was going to make it, we needed an education. In pursuing the goal of achieving an education, I attended ten schools in thirteen years (ranging from low-performing neighborhood schools to private and Montessori). This unique experience gave me my first real lessons in conscious duality and my first experience with psychological tight spaces—the psychological residue of my multiple marginalizations.

The writing of this book is in response to my experiences in academia. Although the pursuit of being educated should be liberating, it continues to bind me with new sophisticated chains such as "scholarship," "minority," "disadvantaged," and "token." To preserve my sanity, I undertook a paradigm shift that demanded a certain amount of self-confidence and security. My journey has taken me from being a round-the-way girl to grassroots activist to carpooling mom to tenured faculty member.

My experiences as a student at predominantly White institutions (PWIs) and a professor at a historically Black college and university (HBCU) have inspired this work. I have experienced "chilly classrooms" and hostile working environments. Because of these experiences, I have learned how to create community nets of safety, protection, and activism to guide me through these perilous journeys. As a mentor, I have spent countless hours training, advising, and guiding students along this treacherous path. As I grew weary in my journey, I felt confident that I was not alone in my need for new and creative coping mechanisms to deal with my multiple marginalizations. I have exhausted all possible resources and have come to realize that I am no longer able to utilize my grandmother's kitchen table for advice, comfort, or even respite. This book was therefore never optional; it is indeed necessary to preserve the "mutiplexities of myself" as I navigate the tight spaces of the academy. This work is also a tool to explore the usefulness of this information and its application to the lives and scholarship of future Black feminist scholars. As Evans (2007) notes,

> Black women's claimed space, negotiation of social contracts, contributions of ideas, and

upholding of social hierarchies all must be explored in future research. Considering marginalized perspectives is essential to evaluation in higher education; alternative narratives offer engaging solutions that address complexities, in new, old, and significant ways. (197)

This work speaks to navigating and negotiating my multiple selves—the roles that are required and expected—as well as my own psychological "conversations" with myself that will allow me to remain sane in an insane world.

ONE

MY JOURNEY BEGINS

> But teaching was about service, giving back to
> one's community. For Black folks teaching—
> educating—was fundamentally political because
> it was rooted in antiracist struggle.
> —bell hooks

Black women have participated in American higher education for more than one hundred years. Despite enduring personal and professional barriers, many have made significant advances and have reaped the benefits of their contributions (Gregory 2001). As a student and now as a faculty member, I also endured many personal and professional barriers in an effort to reach my goals. In doing so, I joined a group of Black women who have struggled to survive while navigating multiple forms of oppression.

Psychologists, jurists, and scientists have documented the multiple types of oppression Black women have experienced in America; however, few have investigated the impact of Black feminist rhetoric on Black feminist academicians. Over the last twenty years, scholarship as provided for engaging in anti-oppressive practices. These movements have also created different ways of knowing, thinking, and being in both academic communities and the Black public sphere. According to Holt (1995),

> the contemporary Black public sphere is partly the creature of the political economy of a global, advanced capitalist order, but in the past it has offered—and may yet again offer—space for critique and transformation of that order. If not, then all this is only idle talk. (328)

Educators and institutions of education operate from and are constructed by social and historical relations of power. Because of this, privileged narrative spaces are constructed for some social groups (dominant culture), and spaces for inequality and subordination are constructed for the "other." According to Foucault (1979), power is not imposed from above; rather, its operation and success depend on consent from below. I never recognized just how powerful power can be until someone used his or her power on me. Power is produced and reproduced in the rituals of everyday life and is ubiquitous. Sitting on the stoop in Philly or riding the El, I had no idea that somewhere someone was attempting to write my story—a story of how a child of a single parent, raised in poverty, would not succeed. This story, my story, is a testament to my sheer will to succeed—to not just survive, but to thrive. And I am not alone in my struggle; Black feminist educators, scholars, and academicians daily negotiate power, navigate oppression, and resist domination. I am not denying that other women of color and White women do not have similar struggles; however, within the sociocultural, political, and historical framework of American society, and given the intricate ramifications of slavery within this country, our positionalities are often situated within psychological tight spaces.

The African proverb "She who learns must also teach" speaks of the importance attached to the role and responsibility of Black women faculty in sharing their knowledge regardless of any oppositions or challenges. Education has been an integral part of the survival and liberation of African Americans since their arrival in the Americas in the seventeenth century (Bennett Jr. 1988; Camp 2004; Franklin and Moss 1994; Gaspar and Hine 1996; Giddings 1984; Harrison 2009; Kolchin 1993; Lerner 1972; Morgan 2004; Sterling 1984; Takaki 1993). Although education was ruled illegal, slaves recognized the importance of basic skills (such as reading and writing) to their freedom and survival. Many slaves risked their lives and created underground schools and systems to teach one another and the next generation.

Black women, familiar with the blatant oppression of slavery and postbellum oppression began to wrestle with being ostracized by White women and

Black male movements. In addition, their relationships with Black men were tainted by the dynamics of sexism, creating an additional barrier for Black women. Time and history reveals the intersectionality (Crenshaw,1995) of oppression for Black women to include racism, sexism, heterosexism, and classism. This matrix of oppression (Hill Collins 1990) has Black feminist scholars caught in the crossfire.

From a long history of advocacy and support, I propose the role of Black women in the academy is shifting due to an increase in the number of us receiving doctoral degrees over the past twenty-five years. Although at many institutions, Black women appear to be an integral part of the ivory tower, they continue to deal with the repercussions of their inclusion. I am not suggesting other faculty of color or White faculty from historically impoverished backgrounds are not experiencing levels of repercussions; however, I have witnessed via personal and professional experiences the heightened level of scrutiny in the tenure and promotion process, as well as the insurmountable service and teaching requirements many Black female faculty have to endure at both PWIs and HBCUs. This, along with the sociocultural and political dimensions of gender "norms" and expected traditional familial roles, has presented complex challenges to Black women. The levels of anxiety we experience as we begin to learn to navigate our role as "outsiders within" is insurmountable for some of my sisters. They finally decide to just give up. Surviving hegemonic institutions of domination will require Black women to learn strategies of resistance to deal with their psychological tight spaces.

Given this background, I wondered how critical discourse analyses (CDA) of *Sister Outsider,* by Audre Lorde, and *Teaching to Transgress,* by bell hooks, create a framework for Black women to be successful in the academy, as well as within the context of a global community. How might the Black feminist rhetoric(s) of Lorde and hooks create a framework for Black feminist scholars at HBCUs to engage in liberatory practices? Would the selected works of Lorde and hooks be useful in creating a professional tool kit for Black feminist scholars' survival at HBCUs?

Throughout history, in order for Black women to survive their multiple marginalities and the resulting psychological tight spaces of their oppression, they relied upon faith, social support, body ownership, and unique defense mechanisms (Daly et al. 1995; Howard-Vital 1989; Jones and Shorter-Gooden 2003; St. Jean and Feagin 1998; Terhune 2007; Wilson 2009). These coping methods and strategies were vital in the lives of Black women. They created spaces of support and encouragement within faith communities, sewing circles, civic/social organizations, and learning communities. These strategies were typically handed down generationally utilizing the rich oral tradition of our ancestors (Bennett Jr. 1988; Daly et al. 1995; Giddings 1984) and were often included in kitchen-table talk, where Black women shared formal and informal warnings and tips on how to navigate the "other" world. These coping methods are now problematized by the shifting nature of oppression, increased class mobility, greater educational achievement, geographic isolation, and a decline in the sense of community being experienced by some African American scholars as a result of their class mobility (Bonilla-Silva 2006; Tatum 1987). This has created a void for Black women—particularly young Black women who are in the academy and other professions—to bring about change, without a foundation in Black feminist rhetoric, critical race feminism (CRF), critical race theory (CRT), and/or Black feminist/womanist epistemologies. Many of these women are serving in the role of educator with decreased access to the wisdom and influence of their elders as a guide.

Through CDA of selected works from hooks and Lorde, I am attempting to create a framework and tool kit for Black feminist educators in the academy. Recognizing the limitations of attempting to research experiences on the surface that many believe to be monolithic, I engage an inquiry that focuses on the works of three Black feminist scholars who are well read and notable across multiple communities. Although hooks, Hill Collins, and Lorde have defining experiences unique to their own circumstances and conditions, collectively they offer a Black feminist rhetoric that is transforming, engaging, and powerful. Clearly there is no one experience in the United States or globally for Black women; however, the rhetoric these women offer exhibits a criticality that transcends time, space, and differences. The commonality of their visions and the intersection of their ideologies provide a space for engaging inquiry to discover a "truth telling" that serves as the road map to the journey of Black women within the global diaspora. It is understood that the diversity of our experiences (based on class, sexual orientation, education, employment) shape the understanding of our identities and lived experiences; however, what is more important, specifically to this work, is the standpoint of Black women, which continues to create spaces for global transformation. This cannot be overlooked. So, through analyzing the works of hooks and Lorde, at my disposal is a key feature of Black feminist thought: "asking the right questions and investigating all dimensions of a Black women standpoint" (Hill Collins 2009, 37).

Moving Black Women to the Forefront

Black women, since the inception of *Ebony, Jet*, and *Essence*, have engaged their elders via popular text. We have filled our kitchen tables with the works of Black writers, and specifically Black feminist writers who have responded to our marginalization through counterhegemonic discourses. However, since the dawn of the Internet and World Wide Web, the explosion of social networking sites, and mediated imagery that is presented across streaming video at the command of the "point and click," of a mouse, many young Black feminist scholars who find themselves as social agents are continuing to experience barriers (Cooper and Gause 2007; Roseboro and Gause 2009).

There are significant contributions from scholars of color, and I believe hooks, Lorde, and Hill Collins—who are considered to be exemplars and luminaries in the field of gender studies, sociology, and the humanities—offer considerable rhetoric(s) in developing a tool kit for negotiating power, navigating oppression, and resisting domination within institutional structures that are filled with White-supremacist capitalist patriarchy (hooks 1994). Black women are continuously looking for their footing on shifting grounds.

Creating new ways of knowing and being is not a new phenomenon for Black women. The work of Alice Walker (1983) and the Combahee River Collective (1983) are examples of attempts by Black women to create new ways of dealing with their marginality. For me and for many other young Black feminist educators/scholars, the works of other Black feminist educators/scholars provide tools and strategies for surviving the marginality that we experience in institutions. As Hill Collins (2009) opines, "as social conditions change, so must the knowledge and practices designed to resist them" (43).

The result of my discourse analysis is compared to my lived experiences as a Black feminist scholar, and areas of convergence and divergence are explored. Finally, these works will be explored to see how they inform the intellectual, spiritual, and psychological development of Black women navigating the politics inherent in institutions of domination. The importance of this work is supported by the vast amount of research conducted on the challenges faced by US Black women in the academy. Research studies have examined the current challenges faced by Black female faculty (Bambara 1970; Beoku-Betts and Njambi 2009; Brown-Glaude 2010; Evans 2007; Gregory 1995; hooks 2004; Hill Collins 1990 2000; Lerner 1973; Sterling 1984) while personal narratives have shared stories of survival and resistance (Brock 2005; Carter-Black 2008; hooks 2004). One study of Black women in the academy working in the United Kingdom grounded their research in the work of hooks, Lorde, and Hill Collins (Burke, Cropper, and Harrison 2000). As Black women are being researched, our experiences continue to change, making it critical that research be continuous. Evans (2007) notes, "African American women's experiences and ideas, though in many ways timeless, are significantly challenged by the complexities of twenty-first-century institutions; as problems change over time, so should solutions" (195).

"Maids of the Academy"

With an increasing number of Black women receiving doctoral degrees, the illusion of progress continues to paint a picture of equality and equity in America. Yet closer examination reveals a hidden picture. Although Black women are increasing in the number of PhDs acquired, there still exists a lack of racial parity. Fields in which Black women receive their terminal degrees (primarily education) and the institutions they work in upon completion continue to be disproportionate in comparison with their White counterparts. Black women work at less prestigious institutions and receive tenure at a rate much lower than their colleagues; they are often clustered in clinical, assistant, instructor, and other "academic apartheid" positions (Gregory 2001). This has led to Black women being utilized as what Harley (2008) terms "maids of academe" and has created "one of the most isolated, underused, and consequently demoralized segments of the academic community" (Carter, as cited in Harley 2008, 21).

Recognizing that "language is also a place of struggle," each woman explored in this book wrote to create spaces of resistance. hooks states that "spaces can be real or imagined. Spaces can tell stories and unfold histories. Spaces can be interrupted, appropriated, and transformed through artistic and literary practice" (as cited in Harding 2004, 159). For bell hooks, it was an issue of class, belonging, and liberation. She was selected for this book primarily for her work on reclaiming the margins as spaces of resistance for African American women. Patricia Hill Collins was selected for this book because of her work on Black women as "outsiders within" and her theoretical framework of Black feminist thought. Finally, Audre Lorde was selected in part for her work on the "many layers of selfhood" as well as the emancipatory nature of her writing.

A CDA of the work of Lorde, hooks, and Hill Collins can provide additional lenses through which Black women in the academy can view themselves. Research continues to support the struggles of Black female faculty at both the micro (tenure and promotion) and macro (institutional barriers) levels. The thoughtful critique of works done by African American feminist scholars can create an additional way of being and knowing the world for Black women in the academy. This book recognizes that "black women intellectuals have laid a vital analytical foundation for a distinctive standpoint on self, community, and society, and in doing so, create a multifaceted, African American women's intellectual tradition" (Hill Collins 2009, 5). This standpoint can assist Black women as we develop our consciousness and could potentially add to the "collective group consciousness" of African American women.

This work is also important as the survival strategies discussed earlier above seem to be reactive and, at times, pathological. Black women cannot continue to survive by reacting to oppression with tools that do not eventually allow us to use, or understand, our condition in a more psychologically healthy way. Black women are in search of survival strategies that are liberatory, allowing us to transcend the psychological constraints we may find ourselves in, and engage the real issues we are struggling with in our daily lives. Part of this liberation will demand an understanding of the critical role voice plays in the struggle from the oppressor; it is a starting point at which many Black women stand, afraid and silenced. In the poem, *A Litany for Survival*, Lorde (1978) addresses this fear:

> And when we speak we are afraid
> our words will not be heard
> nor welcomed
> but when we are silent
> we are still afraid
> so it is better to speak
> remembering
> we were never meant to survive. (32)

In an attempt to address this fear and answer more sophisticated questions, questions our aunts, mothers, and grandmothers may not be able to answer, Black female scholars have searched the literature of those they emulate. As hooks (1996) recounts,

> many times readers come up to me and say, 'I was sitting at home, asking myself those questions and asking myself how I would deal with them, and then I come to something you've written, and you help me understand not only how I got to where I am but how I can move further on.' (818)

This type of critical engagement of literature helps create a standpoint for Black feminist scholars solidifying the importance of theory as it relates to action and beginning to shake the foundation of fear.

There is no monolithic experience for Black women in academia as institutions vary in size, location, and demographics, creating nuances within campus cultures. However, research has demonstrated enough similarities between experiences to justify a standpoint for the experiences of Black women in academia. According to hooks (1996), "Academe is, essentially, a competitive corporate structure. Many of us academics now operate competitively within feminist circles. In an atmosphere of competition, people become more guarded, more defensive, and, frankly, more paranoid" (824). This type of environment, one that creates defensiveness, competition and paranoia, is not healthy for most individuals; however, this environment takes an especially hard toll on Black women in academia (Gregory 1995; Moses 1989). Black women in academe experience additional challenges such as feelings of alienation/isolation, tokenism, cultural taxation, mentoring, service work, internalized oppression; role strain, and psychological and physical health issues (Gregory 2001).

The historical marginalization of Black women across multiple domains in their lives (work, social institutions, academia, and interpersonal) has been well documented, and it has created psychological tight spaces in which African American feminist scholars must learn to navigate (Bambara 1970; Camp 2004; Carroll 1982; Carter-Black 2008; Evans 2007; Giddings

1984; Hill Collins 1990; hooks 1989, 2004; Lorde 2007). Although the scope of this book is limited to Black feminist scholars in the Academy, it is crucial to recognize two important points. Firstly, many of the issues facing Black feminist scholars in the academy overlap the issues facing *all* Black women. However, the role of power in the academy has created a unique culture that demands a variation to the established coping methods. Secondly, all Black women in the academy deal with oppression and marginalization, from professors to administrative and janitorial staff. Although the scope of this book was limited to scholars, I am guided by the words of Angela Davis (1994): "Self-preservation demands that [educated Black women] go among the lowly, illiterate and even the vicious, to who they are bound by ties of race and sex...to reclaim them" (423).

Chapter 2 provides a framework for understanding the historical development of coping methods utilized by Black women both inside, and outside, the academy. This chapter begins with a brief history of Black women and education, Black women in academia and discusses coping methods utilized in both arenas. Chapter 3 discusses the qualitative frameworks that serve as the foundation of this book. CRT and CRF will be explored because of the intersectionality of both theoretical orientations within the context of power. In general terms, power, as a linguistic term, has a variety of interpretations and meanings. What does it mean to have power? Is power based on perception? How does power influence ideologies. Black feminist thought and standpoint theory are explored for the theoretical foundation they provide for exploring the commonalities of oppression and resistance for all Black women.

Chapter 4 explains the use of CDA as a methodology and describes the methods utilized to understand the selected texts of Audre Lorde and bell hooks, as well as provides a biographical "snapshot" of these phenomenal Black feminist educators/scholars. Chapter 5 provides the analyses of Audre Lorde and bell hooks. Chapter 6 examines the knowledge gained for its usefulness as a teaching tool and in developing a framework for dismantling, this old house—the academy. The coping strategies Black women utilize as while engage in their liberatory practice are presented within a developed tool kit. I believe the results presented and discussed will provide Black women a framework to fight against their psychological tight spaces, particularly at HBCUs.

TWO

THE JOURNEY OF MY UNFAMILIAR

Black Women: Oppression and Resistance

This chapter provides a framework for understanding the historical development of coping methods utilized by Black women both inside and outside the academy. This historical backdrop is needed to develop a comprehensive picture of the multiple challenges faced by Black women and the creative responses they formed. Coping methods utilized by Black women have been learned, passed down, or observed in a variety of settings. This chapter provides an opportunity for the reader to increase their understanding of the depth, breadth, and scope of Black women's experience in America.

This chapter contains an abbreviated history of the oppression of US Black women, including resistance strategies created for survival. I provide an overview of some of the pivotal moments of the oppression of Black women and highlight the ways Black women have resisted their marginalization.

Female Slave Narratives

The use of female slaves narratives as a means to provide a snapshot of the types of atrocities experienced during this period of US history has become more popular in Black Feminist Scholarship. Although some well-known names have begun to make it into classroom instruction and mainstream culture (Harriet Tubman and Sojourner Truth), there are several other less known narratives that provide an accurate view of the life of female slaves. Among my favorite are *Harriet Jacobs: Incidents in the Life of a Slave Girl* (Jacobs 2001) and *Our Nig: Sketches from the life of a Free Black* (Wilson 2009). It is primarily from these accounts that I have begun to piece together the depth of oppression facing US Black women during slavery and the creative resistance strategies utilized.

Harriet Jacobs

Linda Brent uses the pseudonym Harriet Jacobs in the retelling of her life as a slave. Her narrative, like many of that time, includes an introduction by a White woman to add credibility for her intended audience, White women, with the hope of galvanizing them into action against slavery. New to Harriet Jacob's slave narrative was the introduction of the

> so-called sentimental novel (sometimes known as the novel of seduction) in order to dramatize her theme of virtue under siege...Her story

focused on the plight of enslaved black women who, as material possessions, were subject to rape by their masters. To satisfy the sexual desires of these men and to increase their wealth by producing more slaves, these hapless women were deprived of any semblance of family, as well as denied a place in the Victorian 'cult of true woman hood' where piety, purity, submissiveness, and domesticity would affirm their proper place in the moral and social order. (Jacobs 2001, vi)

Jacobs' story follows her from her childhood (around the age of seven) until she recognizes that she is, indeed, a slave. Having lost her carefree life, Jacob spends her teen years cleverly circumventing the advances of her master, Dr. Flint.

Harriet Jacob's personal narrative is a palatable tale of the atrocities of lives of Black women during slavery. The oppression during this critical time period came in the form of blatant physical domination as well as control of women's bodies.

This oppression was physically and psychologically aimed at breaking the spirit and souls of Black women through lack of basic needs (food, clothing) as well physical abuse. Harrison (2009) places acts of violence against female slaves into five categories: domestic, sexual, sisterhood, "sistah"-hood, and self. Domestic and sexual violence involved the intimate violence by the slave owner toward the female slave, including the most frequent form of violence, rape. Sisterhood violence describes violence against women (such as mistresses) toward female slaves. "Sistah"-hood violence explores the violence that occurred between female slaves. Self-violence describes the lasting piece of domination against female slaves— internalized violence and fear. Harrison's categorization, although helpful, is not all-inclusive. Her categories are an easy way to view a system whose atrocities and impact are still felt to this day. Objectification of Black women occurred as part of the multiple attacks toward female slaves. This system of objectification created and maintained images of Black women as "mammies" and "jezebels." This system continues to be reified through the imagery provided by the Black public sphere and popular culture.

Resistance strategies during slavery.

It would be naïve to think that all African women endured slavery with strength and resiliency as yet unmatched. Indeed, many female slaves were unable to stand the brutality of the system of slavery and resorted to suicide and others acts of self-mutilation (Bambara 1970). It is those who chose to resist that the author is interested in, and how they chose resistance. Resistance came in many forms and began creating counter-narratives to the hegemonic ideology of slavery. Harrison (2009) discusses five counterhegemonic tactics in her book *Enslaved Women and the Art of Resistance in Antebellum America*: reclaiming dignity and value, fighting back, thinking of ways to escape, consulting religious practitioners, and using herbs, for wellness and protection. Acts of resistance also included spirituality, individual and collective revolution, the use of herbs, and acts of subversion (such as learning to read and write). Part of the strength that allowed female slaves to resist came from strength and knowledge gathered in intimate interactions and support groups, which allowed the resistance to occur. Harrison (2009) writes,

> the women were their own antidotes, the healing agents of one another. Deep within these enslaved daughters of Akan, Igbo, Bambara, Temme, Mende, Fon-Ewe-Yoruba, and Congolese-Angolan women born-free was the cure to the trickster's sugarplum poison. At the core of their being, beneath the layers of multidimensional oppression and violence was a river, and indigenous wellspring of womanist vitality. Domestic, sexual, sister-hood, sistah-hood, and self-violence may have damned these resilient, healing, protesting waters to a trickle; however, it was enough for the women to draw onto push through, press on, and transcend any obstacle in their path.
>
> This wellspring was most evident in them when they gathered at night down by the riverside and away from the watchful eye of their masters...power was best reflected and energized in them when they sang, danced, ring shouted, drummed, conjured, root-worked, educated themselves, affirmed one another, and contemplated and strategized their way to freedom...they communed with this world, and

> pulled from themselves and others resources and
> strategies to resist and transcend violence and
> oppression...They became a river, transforming
> and resilient, signifying to the world that the river
> of the human spirit could neither be contained
> nor forever damned by human oppressors or
> violence. A restless contained and violated river
> eventually unleashes itself in subversive,
> protesting, and rhythmic ways. (147–148)

As Harrison points out, the resistance efforts of Black women were often fueled by the camaraderie of the group. Black women shared with each other ways to get through the unthinkable, and most managed to do so. The importance of these tactics, and what ultimately made them useful is that Black women shared with each other the knowledge they gained over the years (Davis 1983). This method of resistance, the shared wellspring knowledge gained, was invaluable to the survival of slaves. Female slaves choosing to resist in more subversive ways, often used resistance through education; slave women, recognizing the importance of reading and writing, found ways to teach others whatever information they learned. Sometimes this information came in less organized gatherings, and other women went as far as to organize schools:

> In Natchez, Louisiana, there were two schools
> taught by colored teachers. One of these was a
> slave woman who had taught at a midnight
> school for a year. It was opened at eleven or
> twelve o'clock at night, and closed at two o'clock

a.m....Milla Granson, the teacher, learned to read and write from the children of her indulgent master in her old Kentucky home. Her number of scholars was twelve at a time, and when she had taught these to read and write she dismissed them, and again took her apostolic number and brought them up to the extent of her ability, until she had graduated hundreds. A number of them wrote their own passes and started for Canada. (Lerner 1973, 32–33)

Milla is just one of example of how female slaves went to extraordinary lengths to reach out and change their environments. Her simple, yet terrifyingly brave, act of educating slaves left an impact on hundreds of slaves. Her method of resistance was subversive and methodical, yet very effective.

Black female slaves faced physical, psychological, and spiritual oppression at the hands of their masters. The oppression was clear, and often smothering, forcing mothers to make hard choices regarding the politics of their bodies. The ideology of racism based on color was beginning to create the backdrop for the country for years to come. In response to the oppression during slavery, female slaves fought back, planned and executed escapes, participated in rebellions, reclaimed their dignity, created supportive groups, used the legal system, called on their religious upbringing, and utilized education. This shotgun approach to resisting oppression was necessary during this time period, as female slaves could and were assaulted on a daily basis. The use of groups, to support each other, share information and strategize was made possible by the close quarters in which slaves lived. Freedom, and the type of oppression it brought, began a geographic shift within the African American community that called for adjustments in resistance tools and has had long-term implications.

Cult of True Womanhood

Freedom presented a different set of challenges for Black women, who struggled to find their role in the overall advancement of Blacks. The oppression of Blacks began to shift during this period from the physical or geography of containment (Camp 2004) to forms of bondage, such as indentured servitude that presented the illusion of freedom; therefore, during this period, a shift from paternalism to patriarchy occurred by Whites, who felt like they no longer had to implicitly

> justify what seemed only natural, namely, hierarchical societies...Their culture and politics expressed the established social values of the ruling elite; they did not seek to impart those values to the lower classes and to the enslaved or to coerce these populations into sharing their assumptions and priorities. Political discourse and everyday culture...expresse[d] but did not justify social place. (Camp 2004, 17)

This period in history has historical significance. This period sets the stage for the types of long-standing oppression and marginalization I expand upon and investigate throughout this book.

During the highly religious postbellum period, while White women were forming religious groups, Black women formed mutual aid societies to assist other free Blacks. Forty Massachusetts women who formed the Colored Female Religious and Moral Society of Salem formed one of the first of such societies. The group wrote their own regulations and charged dues of a penny per week. These organizations continued to multiply over time and "as a second generation of free women matured, their 'African' societies became 'colored' and 'mutual relief' was broadened to include 'mutual improvement'" (Sterling 1984, 110).

Mutual aid and literary societies

Mutual aid societies acted collectively to provide relief and financial assistance to free Blacks. There were multiple societies that popped up throughout the North with the simple notion that in order to move ahead through these treacherous times, Blacks needed to support each other and become accountable for their role in securing a more stable future. The mutual aid societies were supported in this mission by literary groups, such as the Ohio Literary Ladies Society, whose main purpose was to educate White women about the plight of Blacks in hopes of creating change. These literary groups allowed for "calls for action" by several well-known Black women including: Frances Ellen Watkins (Harper), Isabella Baumfree (Sojourner Truth), and Maria Stewart. All three women, in similarly distinct ways, challenged the status quo of the time period and encouraged Blacks and challenged Whites with impassioned speeches.

Maria Stewart was the first Black American born woman to speak freely, albeit for a short period of time (one year). Her speeches acknowledged the contradiction between the Victorian ethic and biases based on current practices. Her main points called for a recognition of the existence of racism; the encouragement that free Blacks become more active; the importance of the role of mothers as tools to develop the future and impart tools for survival; and the belief that Black women did belong to the "cult," noting that the "cult of true womanhood" started in the Majestic history of African Kings and Queens. Stewart openly challenged this notion that the "cult of true womanhood" only applied to White women. Her impassioned pleas challenged free Blacks to begin whatever small movements toward change that they could. In one particular speech, Stewart stressed the importance of action and education. She states,

> it is of no use for us to sit with our hands folded, hanging our heads like bulrushes, lamenting our wretched condition; but let us make a mighty effort, and arise. Let every female heart become united, a let us raise a fund ourselves; and at the end of one year and a half, we might be able to lay corner-stone for the building of a High School,

that the higher branches of knowledge might be enjoyed by us. (Sterling 1984, 154)

Stewart's "assumptions—what would later become known as modernist thinking—gave Black women a freer rein to express and act upon ideas that liberated them from the oppression of both sex and race" (Giddings 1984, 52). And although the ideas formed did not directly "liberate" Black women from the oppression of both sex and race, they did begin to plant seeds for new ways of being, thinking and knowing.

A more commonly known woman of this era is Isabella Baumfree, a former slave who changed her name to Sojourner Truth, based on her "calling" to go wherever the truth needed to be told. She did not travel along planned routes instead she went wherever she felt "the Spirit" called her (Sterling 1984). In a dialogue with Harriet Beecher Stowe, Truth shares how she received her new name:

The Lord has made me a sign unto this nation, an' I go round a'testifyin', an' showin' their sins agin my people. My name was Isabella; but when I left the house of bondage, I left everything behind. I wa'n't goin' to keep nothin' of Egypt on me, an' so I went to the Lord an' asked him to give me a new name.

And the Lord gave me Sojourner, because I was to travel up an' down the land, showin' the people their sins, an' bein' a sign unto them. Afterward I told the Lord I wanted another name, 'cause everybody else had two names; and the Lord gave me Truth, because I was to declare the truth to the people. (as cited in Sterling 1984, 151)

One of Truth's more well-known speeches, "Ar'n't I a Woman," directly challenged the gender roles and expectations being created by the "cult of true womanhood." Truth asserted, as only she could, that she too had plowed fields, worked as hard as a man, enduring lashings, and yet, wasn't she a woman?

The Evolution of Black Citizenry

The period following reconstruction presented unique challenges for Blacks. From 1914 to 1960 the Black community would deal with issues and opportunities surrounding World Wars I and II, the great depression, the Harlem Renaissance, Northern migration, and the nineteenth amendment. Blacks in general found themselves hopeful about their chance to fully become integrated into American society as full members and citizens.

Both world wars greatly impacted this time period. Blacks, who were hopeful for a chance to become full citizens, found themselves fighting in segregated units, regardless of their eagerness to willingly serve the country. This fight still did not include the rights of Black women who still found themselves on the margins of society. A greater picture was beginning to emerge: that of Black women realizing that not only did they have to fight for their basic human rights based on race, but *within* their race they had to fight for their rights as *women*. As Beale (1969) would later write extensively about, "double jeopardy" was in full effect.

Resistance

As Black women continued to deal with physical and economic oppression, they worked hard to create acts of resistance that would enable them to move forward as a group, including the club movement, education, literature, and opportunities for employment. The founding of the National Association for Colored Women (NACW) is one of the best examples of Black women's ability to maneuver through double oppression. Not wanted in White female societies and forbidden from some Black male organizations, such as the American Negro Academy, whose bylaws stated explicitly that only "men of African descent were to participate," Black women created their own spaces and communities of resistance (Giddings 1984, 116).

The motto of the NACW was "lifting as we climb" and with Mary Church Terrell as its first president, the organization distinguished itself as one of the first national Black organizations to deal with the needs of the race. By 1916, with membership hovering near fifty thousand, the NACW set about its mission of being one of the few vehicles that allowed Black women to gain recognition as "a distinct social and political force" (Giddings 1984, 96). This is a pivotal point in the development of the research and scholarship of Black women as a separate entity to be studied apart from White women and Black men. Anna Julia Cooper put it best when she discussed the opportunities and challenges facing "colored" women in the twentieth century:

> The colored woman of to-day occupies, one may say, a unique position in this country...She is confronted by both a woman question and a race problem, and is as yet an unknown or an unacknowledged factor in both...to be a woman of the Negro race in America, and to be able to grasp the deep significance of the possibilities of the crisis, is to have a heritage, it seems to me, unique in the ages. (as cited in Lerner 1973, 572)

The NACW, like mutual aid societies, became part of the larger club movement of the time. Its founding members were very prestigious; they included the daughter of Frederick Douglas, Ellen Craft, and Frances Ellen Harper. NACW, with all the good it was doing, was still hindered by class. The organization's founding member subscribe to the moral and religious standards of that time, subscribing to middle-class values that went largely unchallenged. Poor Black women still found themselves on the margins without time, resources, or connections to increase their involvement with organizations and have their voices heard. The NACW did not forget about the poor; they did conduct outreach projects, and so on, but historians argue that this form of service was conducted largely because it was one of the few areas in which Black women's organizations were allowed to participate.

Black male/female relationships

The shifting economic ground exacerbated all marital relationships but was extremely difficult on Black male/female relationships. With Black men searching for their elusive "manhood" and Black women making conscious choices to fight for the cause, sometimes at the risk of not marrying, those who did commit to each other struggled through very difficult issues.

Black women wanted Black men to stand up for their rights and the "vileness of White men," but it seemed as though on the topic of Black women's rights, Black men's attitudes regressed to a previous century. Anna Julia Cooper stated: "we need men…who can let their interest and gallantry extend outside the circle of their aesthetic appreciation; men who can be father, brother, a friend to every weak, struggling, unshielded girl" (as cited in Giddings 1984, 114). As Black women searched for their role within the race struggle, and within the home, many took to writing as an act of resistance and liberation.

Write it out

Black women writers during this time wrote with an intensity matched only by their yearning for equality and identity. Although there are many well-known authors of the time, three Black female authors who set the stage for that period and for this book were Jessie Fauset, Nella Larsen, and Zora Neale Hurston. Each of their unique works and genres contributed to the landscape of Black women's "search for self."

During the Harlem Renaissance—a period of rebirth and self-definition for Blacks—it was of ultimate importance that Black women begin the process of defining *themselves* for *themselves*. As Audre Lorde (2007) warned, "If we do not define ourselves for ourselves, we will be defined by others—-for their use and to our detriment" (45). The definition of Black womanhood was whirling in a vortex of images and "it was particularly important that Black women answer the questions, for their image affected how they were perceived—and treated—by society and by their men" (Giddings 1984, 194).

The Writers

Jessie Redmon Fauset (1884–1961) was born outside of Philadelphia to a working-class family. Fauset attended the Philadelphia High School for Girls and hoped to attend the prestigious all women Bryn Mawr college. Bryn Mawr sidestepped this thorny issue by arranging for her to receive a scholarship to Cornell University. While at Cornell, Fauset became the first Black woman to obtain a Phi Beta Kappa key. Fauset's four novels—*There Is Confusion* (1924), *Plum Bun: A Novel without a Moral* (1929), *The Chinaberry Tree: A Novel of American Life* (1931), and *American Style* (1933)—were all written between 1924 and 1933, and they tackled issues surrounding the Black middle class, belonging, and "color mania" in America.

As a precursor for this book, her novel, *Plum Bun*, is most intriguing. It explores the complex issues surrounding a light-skinned Black woman who passes for White, raising salient issues on skin tone, acceptance (within and outside one's community), belonging, and finally, survival. For the protagonist in *Plum Bun*, Angela Murray, passing for White becomes a way of surviving. At the same time it ostracizes her from the Black community, leaving her in some sort of societal purgatory, creating a "tight space," which she undoubtedly had to learn to navigate.

Zora Neale Hurston's (1891–1960) work technically falls outside of the years of the Harlem Renaissance, yet the impact and style of her writing defined the period. Hurston grew up in the all Black town of Eatonville, Florida, and much of her worldview is reflected through this unique upbringing. With being educated at Howard and Columbia University, Hurston's style of writing, with characters whose identities were not reactions to Whites, was not always well received. Her most well-known work, *Their Eyes Were Watching God* (1937), plunged readers into the rural South as they followed Janie through her search for identity. Like in Larsen's work, Janie, who is forced to marry by her grandmother for security reasons, spends her life seeking the freedom in a relationship to just "be." She finds it during the latter part of the book, with a man (Tea Cake) who

> loves her for herself, not for what she represents to him. This is more important than material security or social status, for it allows her sense of self to be freed at last. Her identity is finally able to take shape, critic Mary Helen Washington observed, because she is able to 'throw off the false images which have been thrust upon her.'
> (as cited in Giddings 1984, 193)

Through her brave writing, Hurston sets a framework for discovery and liberation that has lasted to current day.

Nella Larsen (1893–1964) was born to a Danish mother and a Black West Indian father, who died when she was young. Larsen's mother remarried someone of like race, setting the backdrop for Larsen's novels…being the "only"—as Nella grew up as a Black woman in a White family. She attended Fisk University and tried her hand at nursing, but it was her work in the Public Library system in New York that gave her the space to create her first novel, *Quicksand* (1928). Nella, much like her protagonist Helga Crane, struggled with "fitting in"; not feeling comfortable in the South, and yet, not quite fitting in with those in the North. Larsen fell into a category created by her reality—too much White to be Black, but too Black to be White.

Crane, like Larsen, is a product of an interracial relationship and

> the circumstances of her birth present a double-edged identity crisis. Where does she belong?...She feels alienated from 'Negro society,' which, while professing racial pride and disdain for Whites still imitates White values. She is left cold and unfulfilled by the Black bourgeoisie. (Giddings 1984, 192)

When the man Helga loves marries another, she falls into despair and eventually marries a Black minister. Helga, experiencing for the first time emotional and sexual release, comes to realize over time that the freedom she thought she was living in is also an illusion—and she begins to feel trapped by the small town, religious mores, and yearly pregnancies. As with Fauset's characters, Larsen's protagonist feels as if "there is a part of [her] in all of the worlds she has confronted, but she belongs to none of them. And the reader assumes that she will live the rest of her life in mental anguish" (Giddings 1984, 192).

These three Black female writers set the tone for future writers such as hooks and Lorde to explore their creative expression via literature as acts of liberation. Each author's characters assisted her in working out personal dilemmas in her life. The connection between these authors, and me, is also important for this inquiry project. Although I found connections with Fauset, Hurston, and Larsen, it was Fauset's personal story that I was most able to connect with, given that we are from the same area and attended the same high school.

Civil Rights

The civil rights movement was a period of great change and turbulence for all Americans. Hegemonic practices and institutional racism and sexism were now being legally challenged. The role of Black women throughout this movement continued to involve participation in organizations (such as Student Nonviolent Coordinating Committee (SNCC), National Association for the Advancement of Colored People (NAACP), and National Council for Women (NCW), education, and literature. If Black women thought they were fighting hard against images a few decades ago, they found themselves under attack by the role of media and popular culture that began a new assault on Black women through the creation of images and stereotypes (made easier by the increasing access to media by the majority of Americans). Black women were in the middle of their own private war.

Who's your mammie?

The same "fierce single-mindedness" that helped African American women survive through the decades is often labeled aggressiveness, and it has become one of the negative stereotypes reinforced through popular culture. The representation of African Americans in popular culture ranges from omission to overtly and covertly negative stereotypes (asexual mammies, etc.). Although the increased visibility of Blacks in popular culture has been touted as progress, a more critical look reveals the potential negative impact of these images on the Black community. The commodification of Blacks impacts the identity of a culture on a personal and group level (Gause 2008; Giddings 1984; Wallace 1983, 2004). When Black men are represented as "bestial, hyper-aggressive, and hyper-sexualized animals" (Gause 2008, 2), they begin to internalize the lack of value society places on their worth and identity. Media's portrayal of Black men as "less than" has put an additional burden upon Black women who must balance the skills they have developed for survival with the skills necessary to maintain their relationships. Black women began to shoulder another responsibility, the decline of the Black family and the subsequent poverty that followed. Adding to the media milieu was the release of the controversial Moynihan report that attributed Black poverty to the decline of the Black family structure, including a matriarchal family pattern that continued to break the spirit of Black men (Giddings 1984; hooks 1994).

Popular culture embraced the Black matriarch theme, as it reinforced messages of disempowerment for Black men and created the illusion of power for Black women. The now famous character of Madea (created and portrayed by writer and producer Tyler Perry) personifies some of these traits. Madea, a Black female character portrayed by a man, is a no-nonsense

Black matriarch who leads her family in unconventional methods of comedic communication, relationship building, and childrearing. Madea is strong willed, assertive (or aggressive depending on your read), and asexual. Tyler Perry's "drag" portrayal of this Black matriarch is one who needs no one's advice or assistance and seems perfectly content being a one-woman show. Through largely comedic and humorous segments, Perry convinces his audience that Madea is filled with wisdom and has the uncanny ability to solve all the family problems. He also wants his audience to believe that Madea has no weaknesses. This portrayal of Madea, by Perry, adds to the burden of the Black woman's psychological development by providing another image of a Black woman who does not need emotional, spiritual, or sexual support. Tyler Perry in interviews often states that Madea is a composite of the many women from his childhood. He has built a fortune over the past twenty years from this character's humble beginnings on small regional stages throughout the Southeastern part of the United States to now being a dominant screen presence in Hollywood's mediated popular culture. Madea has always challenged non-gendered conformity and racism.

The type of behavior exhibited by Madea could be part of the coping skills Black women have developed to deal with "gendered racism" (Essed 1991). Gendered racism refers to the "racial oppression of Black women that is influenced by narrow and biased views of gender roles" (Shorter-Gooden 2004, 410).

This unique form of racism demands that Black women develop an "armor" to protect them from the outside world.

Black Women in Education

Education was, and continues to be, a recurring act of resistance across historical time periods. Black women found opportunities for change through education both as students in higher education and as founders and teachers of schools. Education was being framed as a "way out" and a "way up." Black women found themselves in the periphery of the Black male movements of the time and were forced into action both within and outside their race. Lucy Laney, Nanne Burroughs, Charlotte Hawkins Brown, and Mary McCleod Bethune (Bethune-Cookman College) founded schools, and teaching became one of the main occupations of Black women.

Education, although viewed as a necessary act of freedom and liberation by Blacks, was threatening to Whites. As a result, many states created laws prohibiting the education of free Blacks. In 1833 Oberlin College took a stand and decided to admit both White women and Blacks on an equal basis. To take advantage of this educational opportunity, Mary Jane Patterson's family moved her and her siblings from North Carolina to Ohio to attend Oberlin. Their decision paid off when, in 1862, she became the first Black woman to receive a college degree (Perkins 1983). Speculation about the amount of pressure, isolation, and rejection she must have experienced during her collegiate career is based on the descriptions Blacks give of their experiences on White campuses today. Most students report feelings of isolation, exclusion, unfair treatment by faculty, and a lack of "social life" (Anderson 1988; Beckham 1988; Boyd 1973; Burrell 1980; Carroll 1982; Dinka, Mazzella, and Pilant 1980; Hughes 1987; Kleinbaum and Kleinbaum 1976; Willie and McCord 1972). Mary Jane Patterson had a successful career as an educational administrator, but she and her sisters never married, perhaps attesting to the fine balance for Black women of higher education, careers, and relationships.

Black women continued to show their ingenuity during this period of time. Faced with additional forms of oppression based in part on the Great Migration and Harlem Renaissance, Black women rose to the occasion. Economically marginalized, fighting sexism by Black men, and being assaulted by media images, Black women fought to take control of their own images and their lives. This fight was about to include the institution they had believed would free them—academia.

Black Women in Academia

The first three Black women to achieve doctoral degrees were Eva B. Dykes, Georgiana R. Simpson, and Sadie T. Mossell Alexander, all in 1921 in different fields—English, Philosophy, German, and Economics (Gregory 2001). During this very difficult period in history, these women managed to navigate a system that was not designed for their success. These "collegiate black women injected their cultural mores into disciplinary epistemology and contributed sophisticated, practical knowledge" that set out to design a blueprint for Black women in academia to follow (Evans 2007, 127). At the very least, it sent a message loud and clear: it *can* be done.

Between 1921 and 1954, there were "over 60 doctoral degrees awarded to black women" and it became clear that

> education mattered and African Americans sought to make it work for them, regardless of the various methods employed to attain it. The doctorate, in the right hands, became a tool for racial justice and equal human rights. When black women gained access to graduate degrees, they infiltrated the academy in hopes of redefining scholarship and rechanneling resources of educational institutions to benefit the historically disenfranchised. (Evans 2007, 138)

This increase has been reflected in the current statistics regarding Black women in academia. Black women, though the most numerous in faculty of women of color in institutions of higher education in the United States, continue to face challenges regarding tenure and promotion.

These statistics regarding Black women in academia continue to create the illusion of progress and paint a picture of equality and equity in America

(Gregory 1995; Harley 2008). Yet closer examination reveals the broader picture. Although there is an increase in the number of Black women being awarded doctoral degrees, there still exists a lack of racial parity. In 2010 7.1 percent of Black women received their terminal degree, yet Blacks make up about 13 percent of the population in the United States. The fields in which Black women receive their terminal degrees and the institutions they work upon completion continue to be disproportionate in comparison with their White counterparts (Carter-Black 2008; Gregory 1995; Hall 2006; Harley 2008). In addition Black women work at less prestigious institutions, receive tenure at a rate much lower than their colleagues, and are often clustered in clinical, assistant, instructor and other "academic apartheid" positions (Contreras 1998). Carter et al. (1998) have named Black women as "one of the most isolated, underused, and consequently demoralized segments of the academic community" (as cited in Harley 2008, 21).

Challenges Facing Black Women in Academia

Alienation and isolation. The overarching theme of the research on challenges facing Black women in academia focused on feelings of alienation and isolation. Black women in academia describe the sense of loss and frustration they often find themselves facing. Alexander and Mohanty (1997) describe these problems of academy as "sense of alienation, dislocation, and marginalization that often accompanies a racialized location with white institutions" (68). Although a large portion of the research focuses on this phenomenon at PWIs, this feeling is also valid at HBCUs. Billingslea-Brown and Gonzales De Allen (2009) found that HBCUs often privilege race over other identities, continuing to leave Black women feeling alienated and isolated.

hooks (1990) uses the term marginalization to describe the outer edges in which Black women live and defines it as "part of the whole but outside the main body" (149). She emphasizes, however, that "despite being located on the margins—an unsafe and risky position for any member of an oppressed group— Black women and other women of color need not consider their place in the academy as one of deprivation solely" (149). hooks (1990) states the following:

> [M]arginality [is] much more than a site of deprivation; in fact...it is also the site of radical possibility, a space of resistance. It was this marginality that I was naming as a central location for the production of a counter-hegemonic discourse that is not just found in words but in habits of being and the way one lives. As such, I was not speaking of a marginality one wishes to lose—to give up or surrender as part of moving into the center—but rather of a site one stays in, clings to even, because it nourishes one's capacity to resist. It offers to one the possibility of radical perspective from which

to see and create, to imagine alternatives, new
worlds. (149–150)

In this interpretation, hooks has seamlessly crossed
over from challenge to coping strategy, cautioning us
that issues viewed from a deficit model can cause
extreme psychological damage. Instead, reclaiming
spaces may provide Black women the capacity to
continue in their efforts to resist and provide a new lens
to see and create new worlds.

Hill Collins (1990) frames this isolation as a
result of Black women's "outsider within" status in
academia. This refers to the feeling of being let in to
certain circles (academia), yet still pushed to the fringes.
We have been given a glimpse into the lives of "others"
but are constantly reminded that we are not organically
from that place. The concept is problematic if Black
women view themselves as needing to be "let in" to
other circles, and so on, because this sets up
oppositional thinking. In her book *Black Feminist
Thought* (1990), Hill Collins explores this oppositional
thinking in her three core themes (meaning of self-
definition and self-valuation, the interlocking nature of
oppression, and the construct of dichotomous
difference).

According to Hill Collins (1990), "a careful
review of the emerging Black feminist literature reveals
that many Black intellectuals, especially those in touch
with how they have been marginalized in academic
settings, tap this standpoint in producing distinctive

analysis of race, class, and gender" (104). Referencing the work of Zora Neal Hurston, E. Frances White, and bell hooks, Hill Collins provides a theoretical framework to support hooks's position that Black women reclaim their spaces and utilize the knowledge found there to reimagine their worlds. According to Hill Collins, this type of knowledge creation has in fact been happening for generations, it just has not been viewed as "valid knowledge"—both in mainstream culture and in academia. Describing knowledge production and validation, Hill Collins (1990) states,

> These "radical perspectives" are often blocked within academia and not valued as knowledge. In institutions of higher education, knowledge claims have been traditionally validated by White men. Even though Black women have been producing similar knowledge for generations, the suppression of this knowledge through the continuance of a hegemonic discourse ultimately restricts Black women access to the true inner circles of academia. Black women included in the academy (those with "academic credentials") find themselves caught between using their authority to attempt to promote new knowledge claims of Black women, and recognizing their potential status as 'tokens of the academy,' put in place in an attempt to accept a few 'safe' outsiders. (272)

A hegemonic discourse of knowledge production and validation creates a silencing of women that promotes "the cultural phenomenon of invisibility, both racial and gendered" (Wallace 2004, 225). Women become relegated to the margins, instantly becoming the "other," defined by Lorde (2007) as "the outsider whose experience and tradition is too 'alien' to comprehend" (117). According to Wallace (2004), women of color have an additional layer of being an outsider, from men and from White women. This has left women of color as "the other of the other." Lorde tackles the topic of "other" in her work *Sister Outsider* (2007) while recognizing the marginalized status of Black women; she demands that we not forget that Black women are ultimately responsible for saving Black women and this work will be highly political.

Although slightly different in name, and with slight nuances in theory, no matter what you call it—the result is the same, Black feminist scholars in academe are in fight to save themselves, and by way of the NACW's motto "lifting as we climb," to provide safe locations and strategies for Black students on campus and for each other. We continue to be in a fight to find, define, and defend ourselves.

Cultural taxation. Amado Padilla (1994) introduced the concept of "cultural taxation" to describe the extra burden of additional responsibilities placed upon minority faculty because of their racial, ethnic, and/or gender group memberships. These responsibilities include serving on numerous committees, mentoring larger numbers of students, and serving as the "departmental experts" for their particular gender or ethnic group. These additional expectations for underrepresented faculty, which are not placed as heavily upon White faculty, can impede career progress and may result in psychological problems.

This challenge is evident for Black women in academia, both at PWIs and HBCUs. Black women find themselves "targeted" as the expert, the representative voice for race and gender, the diversity on the search committee, and so on. This phenomenon of cultural taxation has also been discussed as "racial tokenism" by Kelly (2007) during his study of Black teachers as "tokens" in school settings. His research expanded upon the work of Kanter's (1977) theory of tokenism, delineating similar parameters for tokenized Black women in academia, in particular "performance pressure, boundary heightening, and role entrapment" (Kelly 2007, 249). This same phenomenon has been termed "race fatigue" by Turner (2002) Tokenism of Black women in academia is problematized by the negative media images, further pushing Black women into the margins of the Ivory Tower, and compounding their alienation and isolation (Beoku-Betts and Njambi 2009).

The effects of "cultural taxation" are also compounded by the amount of mentoring and service work Black women in academia must conduct. Black women faculty are often sought out by students to act as mentors, reducing the amount of time allotted for scholarly work and creating very tough choices (Carter-

Black 2008; Gregory 1995; Harley 2008). The historical ideology of collectivism held by most Black women in academe is grounded in African and African American traditions (such as the NACW's motto of "lifting as we climb"). This ideology forces Black women faculty to be available to others, as a moral choice. The predicament this creates, however, is one of extinction of Black women faculty due to lack of scholarly progress. Thomas and Hollenshead (2001) note that

> another unwritten rule that Black women and other women of color faculty members often find difficult to address is that one must protect one's time from service work and unlimited interactions with students at all costs, especially if one is not tenured. The conflict in this regard is particularly magnified for women of color when they feel that students of color need their assistance or that specific committees need their voice and representation. (173)

Balancing expectations and navigating competing ideologies is psychologically and physically exhausting. Black women faculty also struggle with guilt associated with "protecting their time" because they recognize that someone "lifted them as they climbed."

Balancing time and responsibilities is not limited to duties at work for Black women in academia. They also struggle with "role strain," balancing the demands of multiple roles and expectations, such as career, family, and church responsibilities (Wilson and

Miller 2002). Role strain can have an impact on Black women in academia as "we constantly have to 'struggle to maintain an integrated sense of self' whilst simultaneously making connections to the concrete material realities of being Black and female" (Burke et al. 2000, 307).

Internalized oppression. Black women in academia are also caught in what Evans (2007) terms the "politics of respectability." Black women often feel additional pressure to prove themselves worthy or better than their colleagues. This viewpoint originates from the understanding that

> excellence is at once repressive and compelling: while buying into ideas of excellence reifies the trappings of ego and merit, it is nonetheless necessary to demonstrate that achievement is commonplace in black women's collegiate history so that when other scholars do excel, it is seen as normative rather than exceptional. (Evans 2007, 210)

Interestingly, Black women are still caught in the conundrum of seeking liberation via the processes that oppress and bind. We need to be constantly reminded that "The master's tools will never dismantle the master's house" (Lorde 2007).

The desire of Black women to prove their equality is an indicator an internalized oppression, which has seeped so far into the psyche of Black women. Many Black women who claim to be "free" are instead courting the illusion of freedom. Carter-Black (2008) has noted in her research that one remnant of this illusion is evidenced by the self-imposed doubts of Black women, which last for years in spite of their accomplishments. The challenges raised above lead to serious physical and psychological health problems for Black women in academia. This passion for teaching, coupled with alienation/isolation, mentoring, role strain, and so on, has resulted in a disproportionate amount of hypertension, heart disease, and depression among Black women faculty (Harley 2008).

Coping Strategies of Black Women in Academia

The challenges to Black women in academia have been met with creative forms of resistance. Some of these resistance strategies carry over from slavery and have been adapted to fit new conditions. They include resiliency, building community, defiance, religion, and mentoring (Gregory 1995, 2001; Thomas and Hollenshead 2001). I situate the coping strategies Black women utilize to survive within a historical, sociocultural, and political context. Ultimately, I seek to alleviate the experiences young Black women have while reacting to power, oppression, and domination with tools that do not eventually allow us "make sense" of our condition in healthy ways. In no way do I speak for all Black women; however, many of the Black women I encounter within my higher education community are in search of survival strategies that will be liberatory, particularly those that will allow us to transcend the multiple constraints that imprison our being.

Resiliency. One of the coping strategies utilized by Black women in academia has been their resiliency. Resiliency theory

> focuses on the fact that individuals with multiple risk factors in their lives are able to triumph over their challenges and do well in spite of the predictions of experts. For African American women resilience is the ability to multi-task, to solve problems, to have a feeling of responsibility and able to make a difference (i.e. internal locus of control), and the use of spiritual beliefs as a support. To truly have resilience requires confidence and hard work, as demonstrated by African American women faculty. (Burke et al. 2000, 298)

Resiliency theory does an excellent job noting select traits that have created a picture of competence and success to allow Black women to physically stay in academia, but it negates to probe further into the underlying mental and physical results of such "resilience." This is an area in need of more, and continuous, research.

Building community. There is a portion of research that speaks to the creation and importance of communities as a tool for resistance and survival (Brock 2005; Brown-Glaude 2010; Shorter-Gooden 2004). As noted earlier, evidence of Black women establishing communities of resistance can be traced all the way back to slavery when women gathered by the river or in the fields to share strategies, sing spirituals, and uplift one another. This strategy has been termed "coalition building" (Gregory 1995), creating "alternative communities" (Brown-Glaude 2010), and "support groups" (Gregory 1995). Regardless of the name, the goal was the same—survival through sharing of information and knowledge in supportive environments. The opportunity to share while being supported is a critical part of the success of Black women in academia, while addressing the political nature of their oppression falls in line with Black feminism, especially if it translates into action.

Harley (2008) presents the importance of gathering as being therapeutic for Black women. She states:

> They talk with each other about their experiences and challenges. Then, they strategize about ways to respond and how to examine the pros and cons of various situations. In many ways networking is therapeutic and African American faculty members act as "kitchen divas" (internal citation omitted) for each other in which they gather support and strengthen each other. (27)

This type of support, rooted in slavery and trace throughout the history of Black women, is vital to their success and mental and spiritual health. In addition,

Black women have undertaken "Courageous Collaborations" (Brown-Glaude 2010) to transform the culture of a university. The study of Black faculty at the University of Maryland emphasized their use of "their intellectual commitments to intersectionality as a means to transform the campus climate by changing the campus curriculum and creating alternative communities" (803). The responsibility of educating the oppressor, in this scenario, still lies with the oppressed—which is problematic. Another issue to consider is when there are not enough Black women on campus to sit at the kitchen table, what if the institution is geographically isolated?

Addressing this issue, Shorter-Gooden (2004) found that geographic isolation allowed for fewer opportunities to utilize the external resource she terms "leaning on shoulders." It refers to "relying on resources outside of oneself [and is] a strategy of developing and using social support as a way of coping with the stress of racial or gender bias" (417). Social support can come from partners, spouses, sisters, and/or close knit groups of friends. Support can be emotional, but it can also be an opportunity for political activism.

The Combahee River Collective (1983) was formed in 1974 by a group of African American feminists that were "actively committed to struggling against racial, sexual, heterosexual, and class oppression" (210). The members of the Combahee River Collective recognize, what so many African

American women attempt to brush aside, that "the psychological toll of being a Black woman…can never be underestimated. There is a very low value placed upon Black women's psyches in this society, which is both racist and sexist" (215). Through their gathering, they built a critical community that provided the support necessary to address the attacks on their psyches.

Defiance. Selecting when and how to defy the power structure has been an intergenerational tool of resistance throughout the Black community (Carter-Black 2008). Defiance has also been shown to be an effective tool of resistance, knowing when to speak and the power of words. Burke et al. (2000) describe defiance "as central to the process of change" (307) and should be done with collaboration and support.

Mentoring. As mentioned earlier as a challenge, mentoring plays a large role for Black women in academia. What is taxing for them as mentors can be helpful as mentees allowing them to develop "creative strategies to find and develop mentorship opportunities outside their academic units, thereby creating communities of resistance" (Thomas and Hoollenshead 2001, 173), described earlier as necessary and productive.

The challenges facing Black women in academe include isolation/alienation, mentoring, and internalized oppression. In response to these challenges, Black women have created communities, networked, exhibited acts of defiance, and utilized their faith. These methods, although helpful, do not address the psychological residue of the resiliency of Black women. Additional coping methods will be necessary to deal with upcoming challenges.

Resistance. African American women continued to develop skills to assist them in their need to be constantly on guard. The impact of the historical marginalization and victimization of Black women is often overlooked, and adds to their unique psychological stress. The Black feminist movement allowed Black women a forum to share their unique stories and histories—stories and histories that were not being heard in feminist circles. Black groups such as the Black Panther Party and The Back to Africa Movement (MOVE) allowed Black women an opportunity to combat racism but not through strong leadership roles. These roles were reserved for men. Living on the edge of two worlds—race and sex— demands creativity and ingenuity for survival, yet is often overlooked by the literature. The unique intersection of racism and sexism is explored in Beale's work on what she has termed "double jeopardy." Although Beale expanded the field of research on this "double jeopardy"—being Black and being a woman— the research is still limited on how African American women *cope* with their unique societal role.

Shorter-Gooden (2004) attempted to answer this question in her research on how African American women cope with the stress of racism and sexism. In a qualitative study done as part of the African American

Women's Voices Project, Shorter-Gooden and Jones distributed questionnaires to African American women hoping to find a clue to the answer of how they manage to cope with the "gendered racism" they encounter daily. She uncovered several main themes: resting on faith, standing on shoulders, valuing oneself, leaning on shoulders, role-flexing, avoiding, and fighting back.

Faith. One coping method I was not surprised to read about was "resting on faith." Throughout the literature, I found several references on the importance of spirituality and/or religion as a coping method (Shorter-Gooden 2004; Tatum 1987; Terhune 2007). It is important to distinguish between spirituality and religion, as they are very unique entities. Although they can overlap each other, they can also stand distinctly on their own.

The role of the church has always played a prominent role in the lives of African Americans. Historically, the Black church provided the only opportunities and information regarding political leadership, education, and finances for African Americans. Church-raised leaders often promised that equality and "freedom" would come through nonviolent resistance or would be a reward on "the other side." Demanding equality, not equity, early church movements pushed for basic civil rights. The role of the Black church has undergone a shift. Middle-class Blacks are generally less active and reliant on the church than their parents were, attributing their successes to meritocracy. There is a still a pocket of

African Americans who fully rely on the church to assist them in dealing with racism. For the "gendered racism" African American women contend with, "resting on faith" continues to be a key coping mechanism.

For some Black women heavily involved in the church, Black theology begins to play a major role in their ability not only to survive but to thrive. According to Cone (1970), "in Black Theology, Black people are encouraged to revolt against the structures of white societal and political power by affirming blackness" (44). This message of affirmation and Black liberation as "the emancipation of the minds and souls of black people from white definitions of black humanity" (62) is crucial in Black women's ability to continue to cope with their marginalization and oppression. As a theology "of and for the black community" (23), Black theology believes in the importance of the community as a backdrop for liberation. This sense of community provides an opportunity for Black women to share their concerns and strategies regarding their oppression. Black women who live in geographically isolated areas face additional challenges in their search for coping methods.

Social Support. Terhune (2007) writes extensively about how African American women cope in isolation. In her study, she interviewed African American women living in Oregon about their experiences. Her findings indicated that African American women living in isolation face a variety of obstacles in their effort to cope and adjust to a potentially hostile environment. According to Terhune (2007), "Black women's lives are inextricably linked to racism, sexism and classism…[which] becomes more prominent when positioned in a predominately White environment, specifically one with a history of exclusion and prejudice" (561). Although Terhune was referring to the geographical location of her subjects, as mentioned earlier, this type of alienation is applicable to Black women in the academy.

One of the challenges of living in isolation is that it provides fewer opportunities to utilize the external resource reported by Shorter-Gooden (2004) of "leaning on shoulders." "Leaning on shoulders" refers to "relying on resources outside of oneself [and is] a strategy of developing and using social support as a way of coping with the stress of racial or gender bias" (417). Social support can come from partners, spouses, sisters, and/or close knit groups of friends. Support can be emotional, but it can also be an opportunity for political activism.

The need for social support extends to African American mothers who may be dealing with an additional layer of stress regarding the tough choices they have made for their children. Choices regarding preschool, neighborhood, playgroups, and afterschool activities are heavily weighed decisions for most mothers. For African American mothers, however, these decisions are additionally layered with concern regarding the psychological well-being of their children. Hill Collins (1990) discusses the unique role of Black mothers as it relates to raising their daughters, when she notes that "Black mothers of daughters face a troubling dilemma. On one hand, to ensure their daughters' physical survival, mothers must teach them to fit into systems of oppression" (123).

Passing it on. Tatum (1987) has examined the tough choice of mothering as it relates to housing in her landmark book, *Assimilation Blues: Black families in White communities: Who Succeeds and Why?* Black mothers who choose to live in White neighborhoods (primarily for safety and quality of schools) must deal with the trade-off of a potential lack of cultural rootedness and the fallout of assimilation. Tatum (1987) discusses this price of assimilation for African American families noting that many African Americans struggle with the concept of biculturalism daily, adjusting or assimilating to both worlds in which they must function. She asserts that "black parents have to guide their children through conflicting developmental tasks during which the child must internalize the dominant views of our society and at the same time learn to recognize and reach his own potentialities" (14). In short, Black parents (most often Black mothers) have the tasks of "providing for the child's basic needs...but in addition Black mothers are almost always involved in socializing their girls and boys to cope with the reality of racism...particularly if they are raising children in predominantly non-Black areas" (Tatum 1987, 10).

It is well documented that Black women have a history of oppression in the United States, and as a result have learned creating methods of resistance. These methods started during slavery and have morphed to match the changing forms of oppression. Methods are often handed down from mother to daughter through a rich oral tradition. The academy presented a new challenge. With fewer Black women's experiences to share, the journey inevitably became a lonely and geographically and mentally isolated one.

THREE

CREATING A FRAMEWORK

Over the last twenty years critical race feminism (CRF) and critical race theory (CRT) has provided scholarship for engaging in antioppressive practices. These movements have also created different ways of knowing, thinking, and being, which have acknowledged the creativity and determination of Black women. These theoretical orientations provide the frame for the house I am attempting to build. Although some may be explained in more detail than others, each piece is an important part of the larger picture. This chapter opens with critical race feminism and critical race theory, and follows up with an in-depth discussion of Black feminist thought and standpoint theory.

Critical Race Theory

CRT is a movement with intellectual underpinnings found in the works of Derrick Bell, Robert Cover, A. Leon Higginbotham Jr., Kimberle Crenshaw, and other progressive intellectuals. The development of CRT grew out of the works of legal scholars and researchers of color who embraced tenets of CLS. Its focus: to confront critically the historical complicity and centrality of law upholding White supremacy and hierarchies of gender, race, class, and sexual orientation. Learning to look critically at race relations is a key part of CRT. Examining everyday interactions, and finding the racial component in them, can help move the racial equality cause forward perhaps more than a simplistic "color blind" approach. Looking carefully at what sociologists call microaggressions can help to see the true extent of racism in the United States. And through critical analysis, it is hoped people can begin to work past issues of race, hegemony, oppression, and domination. Although CRT began within the legal profession—and legal professor Derrick Bell, easily the most important thinker within the movement—it has since spread to many other disciplines. Educators may find CRT very important to their understanding of classroom dynamics, academic testing, and curriculum bias. People involved in the political sphere may find CRT useful in understand voting discrepancies, race-based campaigning, and other issues.

One of the more interesting recent developments in CRT is a questioning of the normative acceptance of "Whiteness." CRT looks at such things as how certain groups—the Irish, for example—began as an "othered" category, before "becoming" White. It looks at how racial pride in being White can manifest in acceptable ways and how it can manifest as White superiority. Additionally, it may consider what Whites can legitimately do to assist the critical examination of race without abusing their position of power.

CRT seeks to examine policies and laws on the juridical administration of justice, as well as the "ways in which race and racial power are constructed and represented in American legal culture and, more generally, in American society as a whole" (Crenshaw, Gotanda, Peller, and Thomas 1995, xiii). Although there are subtleties within CRT, there are two distinct features that unify it: the creation of White supremacy as a tool in the hegemonic oppression of people of color and the importance of not just understanding systems of oppression but working toward changing them. Hill Collins borrows for Black Feminist Thought the notion within CRT that we must be working against systems of oppression, to change the status quo.

Critical Race Feminism

CRF is a genre of scholarship evolving from the writings of three hundred women of color who teach in legal academia. This work examines the intersection of gender, race, and class within a legal and/or multidisciplinary context. It has roots in CRT and Critical Legal Studies (CLS).

Legal scholar Regina Austin's 1989 article, "Sapphire Bound!" calls for minority female scholars in the legal field to straightforwardly, unapologetically, and strategically use their intellectual pursuits to advocate on behalf of poor and working-class minority women. At the risk of being stereotypically identified and labeled as overly aggressive, overbearing, loud, audacious, or in other words, the "angry Black woman," Austin encourages minority female scholars to redefine the Sapphire stereotype to testify to the social and political circumstances impacting minority women. She believes that legal scholars, like herself, embody the necessary attitude and agency it takes to bear the burden of collective struggle alongside, and on behalf of, other minority women.

Black Feminist Thought—Critical Social Theory
Patricia Hill Collins: Black Feminist Thought

Dealing with the historical oppression and marginalization of Black women demands an emancipatory theoretical orientation—one that recognizes that Black women have shared experiences navigating the world, from slavery to present. According to Hill Collins (1990),

> all African American women share the common experience of being Black women in a society that denigrates women of African descent. This commonality of experience suggests that certain characteristic themes will be prominent in a Black women's standpoint. (22)

This suggests there are elements of a Black woman's life that she will have in common with another Black woman based solely on their lived experiences. Again, recognizing and acknowledging that there is no monolithic Black experience for women, Black feminist thought asserts the validity that portions of a collective experience have impacted the epistemological and ontological viewpoints of Black women.

One of the core themes Hill Collins elaborates on is "legacy of struggle," which refers to the idea that all Black women should have some idea of what it is like to struggle in a White male-dominated world. She goes on to acknowledge that in spite of the core themes Black women will share, it is prudent to acknowledge that "diversity among Black women produces different concrete experiences that in turn shape various reactions to the core themes" (Hill Collins 1990, 23).

These shared experiences create an epistemology that is defined as Hill Collins (1990) as "the study of the philosophical problems in concepts of knowledge and truth" (202). Part of the need for a Black feminist epistemology is based on how knowledge and truth have been set up. Typically White males have determined what is valid as knowledge and what the world will consider to be true. This hegemonic ideology has subjugated the voices of *all* women, as well as the unique experiences of Black women. In her quest to study Black women, Hill Collins (1990) shares her frustration at not being adequately prepared as a researcher to study "the subjugated knowledge of a Black women's standpoint" because Black women "like other subordinate groups…have not only developed a distinctive Black women's standpoint, but have done so by using alternative ways of producing and validating knowledge" (202).

Black feminist thought was birthed from Black movements such as Black nationalism and critical social theories such as feminist theory, CRF, CRT, and standpoint theory. Black nationalism (which views Black people as a "nation"—or one "people") helped inform Black feminist thought, through omission of Black women. Recognizing this omission, Black feminist thought realizes the importance of celebrating, owning, and sharing the talents of groups that has been historically ignored. Main leaders and supporters of Black Nationalism are historically sexist and cannot see their heterosexual, male privilege as they attempt to rewrite Black history through their lens. Feminism, CRT and standpoint theory each contributed heavily to the formation of Black feminist thought, because even though the foundation was shared, each theory, in and of itself did not adequately meet the unique needs of Black women. Feminist theory developed in resistance to male domination and began with Betty Friedan's well-known work, *The Feminine Mystique* (1963). In this work, Friedan compares the lives of housewives to that of prisoners, confined in gilded cages but with no freedom to act or make decisions. Friedan's work ignores women who were not middle class, which at the time included the majority of Black women. Her views on domesticity and being "kept" did not apply to the women who *needed* to work outside of the home.

Black feminist thought as a CST is still much needed as Black women continue to struggle within and against several movements whose very wording is under attack (Afrocentrism, Feminism, Black). Within this backdrop, it becomes perhaps even more crucial that Black women recognize "that we are a unique group, set undeniably apart because of race and sex with a unique set of challenges" (as cited in Hill Collins 2009, 25). Black feminist thought does not seek to be separatist; indeed it recognizes that there exists overlap between Black feminist thought and other theories. However, the distinctive nature of Black feminist thought is shaped by the convergence of its six distinguishing features: the dialectical relationship between Black women's oppression and activism, US Black women's standpoint, connections between Black feminist practice thought and Black feminist practice, dialogical practices and Black women intellectuals, Black feminism as dynamic and changing, and the relationship between Black feminist thought and other social justice projects (Hill Collins 2009).

Distinguishing Features of Black Feminist Thought

The dialectical relationship between Black women's oppression and activism. Black women's activism would not be necessary if not for the many forms of oppression facing Black women. It is this dialectical relationship—the very existence and sustainability of a movement and theoretical orientation that only exists because of the oppression its fighting—

that creates a unique position for Black women's activism. In addition, US Black women's movements fight against the contradictions of supposedly basic human rights of all US citizens: the right for equality, freedom, and justice. These rights historically have been divvied up in unjust ways, leaving US Black women sometimes not only questioning "Ar'n't I a woman?" but also wondering "Ar'n't I a citizen?"

Black women's standpoint. This dialectical relationship amid the intersectionality of oppression creates the second distinguishing feature of Black feminist thought, a Black woman standpoint. There exists a tension between the experiences and ideas of Black women and Black feminist thought. Although there is no monolithic experience for Black women, there is a commonality of experiences resulting in a unique standpoint for Black women. Hill Collins (2009) states that

> despite differences of age, sexual orientation, social class, region, and religion U.S. Black women encounter societal practices that restrict us to inferior housing, neighborhoods, schools, jobs, and public treatment and hide this differential consideration behind an array of common beliefs about Black women's intelligence, work habits, and sexuality. (29)

Given the varied perception of these shared experiences, Black feminism is charged with coming up with diverse approaches to these common themes. For example, depending on class, experiences with racism may take various forms. A charge within Black feminism is to allow the space for multiple approaches to grow and be supported.

Black feminist thought and practice. Connecting the practice of Black feminism and Black feminist thought becomes the third distinguishing feature. The relationship between action and thought is not at odds; instead one informs the other. According to Hill Collins (2009), Black feminist thought leads to Black activism:

> A dialogical relationship suggests that changes in thinking may be accompanied by changed actions and that altered experiences may in turn stimulate a change consciousness. For U.S. Black women as a collectivity, the struggle for a self-defined Black feminism occurs through an ongoing dialogue whereby action and thought inform one another. (34)

Within this framework, Hill Collins asserts that knowledge is not enough; it is the action tied to that knowledge with the goal of creating change that will better the experiences of Black women.

Dialogical practices and Black women intellectuals. Acknowledging the existence of a Black woman's standpoint is useless if it is not then critically analyzed for its usefulness in creating or promoting social change. Black women, being historically denied access to formal education, created different ways of knowing and acts of resistance based on their lived experiences at that moment. This allows for the recognition of at least two types of knowledge—commonplace and specialized. Commonplace knowledge exists in the form of "everyday" knowledge that Black women share with each other, such as "how to style our hair, characteristics of 'good' Black men, strategies for dealing with White folks, and skills of how to 'get over'" (Hill Collins 2009, 38). It is my assertion that as a result of this inquiry project, we will find this commonplace knowledge is less accessible for geographically isolated (typically as a result of class mobility) Black women. Specialized knowledge refers to "experts or specialists who participate in and merge from a group...whether working-class, or middle-class, educated or not, famous or everyday" (Hill Collins 2009, 38).

The role of Black women intellectuals in Black feminist thought. The role of Black women intellectuals as central to Black feminist thought is important for the following four reasons: shared experiences, personal investment, self-definition for empowerment, and building collaboration.

Shared experiences. Black women have unique vantage points based on our *experiences* as Black women. As such, we are able to offer critical insights as members of an oppressed group regarding our oppression. According to Hill Collins, this does not mean that other groups are not able to participate in Black feminism; however, it does mean that "the primary responsibility for defining one's own reality lies with the people who live that reality, who actually *have* [emphasis added] those experiences" (39).

Personal investment. Black women intellectuals are more likely to be committed to staying with struggles when others who are less personally invested may be tempted to walk away. Hill Collins discussed the importance of recognizing the relationship between advocacy and personal experiences. She contends that over the long haul, Black women will always remain invested in their liberation.

Self-definition for empowerment. Black women intellectuals are responsible for participating in the ongoing quest for self-definition necessary for empowerment. Hill Collins (2009) states:

> Black feminist thought cannot challenge intersecting oppressions without empowering African American women. Because self-definition is key to individual and group empowerment, ceding the power of self-definition to other groups, no matter how well-meaning or supportive of Black women they may be, in essence replicates existing power hierarchies. (40)

This process of self-definition is another key aspect of this inquiry project, as I seek to rearticulate and reevaluate my role as a Black woman intellectual within Black feminism.

Building collaborations. The last reason why Black women intellectuals are a key component of Black feminist thought is that "we alone can foster the group autonomy that fosters effective coalitions with other groups" (Hill Collins 2009, 40). Collaboration will be necessary among the varying types of Black women intellectuals to create coalitions with other social justice projects. As described above, the role of Black women intellectuals plays a central feature in the creation and sustainability of Black feminist thought.

Black feminism as dynamic and changing.
Another distinguishing feature of Black feminist thought concerns the dynamic nature of social movements. Black feminist thought and activism does not occur in a vacuum; instead it is creating and recreating itself in a vortex of change. Put succinctly, "as social conditions change, so must the knowledge and practices designed to resist them" (Hill Collins 2009, 43). In particular, this feature addresses a component of this inquiry project, namely the impact of the shifting nature of oppression and geographical isolation on Black women intellectuals:

> Under current conditions, some Black women thinkers have lost contact with Black feminist practice. Conversely, the changed social conditions under which U.S. Black women now come to womanhood—class-segregated neighborhoods, some integrated, far more not— place Black women of different social classes *in entirely new relationships with one another* [emphasis added]. (Hill Collins 2009, 43)

And it is within these "entirely new relationships" that another danger exists: "the potential isolation of individual thinkers from Black women's collective experiences—lack of access to other U.S. Black women and to Black women's communities" (Hill Collins 2009, 45). This lack of access to other US Black women and/or Black communities creates a void for Black women intellectuals of both types to share strategies for navigating institutions of domination.

Black feminist thought and social justice.
The final distinguishing feature of Black feminist thought is its role with other social justice projects. Black feminist thought does not seek to be in competition with other social justice causes. Instead, it recognizes that "without a commitment to human solidarity and social justice...and political movement—whether Black nationalist, feminist, or antielitist—may be doomed to ultimate failure" (Hill Collins 2009, 47). Black feminism does not seek to compete with Womanist theory, Africana Womanism, or Feminist theory; instead, it recognizes the role of Black Feminism as ultimately humanist.

It is Hill Collins's charge to utilize this knowledge as a survival and liberation tool that intrigues me most for this project. Hill Collins suggests that Black women recognize our "outsider within" status as the illusion of access within certain circles, only still to find ourselves pushed to the outside. This concept is connected to hooks's view of using the margins as radical spaces of openness and my idea of the psychological tight spaces that are produced as Black women constantly navigate their "selves." Learning from our "outsider within" status becomes a second major area of exploration in my project; it will provide additional tools for navigating hegemonic institutions of domination that I, and the majority of other Black feminist scholars, did not learn at our grandmother's kitchen table.

FOUR

MY JOURNEY'S ROADMAP

This chapter explores the role of discourse at the macro level in creating social practices and tools that are being utilized by Black women. The chapter covers a broad overview of my research paradigm: a description of discourse, discourse analysis, and critical discourse analysis (CDA), as well as a description of the methods selected and my positionality within this book.

While journeying through my life and talking to myself, I began the process of deconstructing all I had ever been taught in school. I found myself finally questioning the "institution" of education and all the curricula I had been fed over the years. Prior to writing this book, I spent forty-eight years as a "model" student. I did not question my teachers or the information they presented. I guess I always trusted their pedagogy and practices. Having been told by my community and family, "to get a good education, so you can have all the things you want by getting a great job," I thought obedience was part of the process.

Entering higher education, I continued to play the game until I entered graduate school. I began conquering this demon throughout my Masters program, when my advisor would assign papers and not give us page limits. I remember this so vividly because it shattered my viewpoint on education. His rationale: "If I tell you how long to make the paper, that's how long you'll write. Your paper needs to be long enough to convey your point, period." I could no longer count words to make the magic word limit, and, if necessary, add any fluff. I adjusted to the "new way" of writing papers, completed my program and graduated.

The systemic institutional practice of just doing enough to meet the standard and not really engaging in scholarly discourse and research reared its ugly head again. After forty-eight credits of course work, comprehensive questions, and a proposal, I thought I had conquered my own need for mastering a system that stifled my voice and crippled my very own thoughts. I began to acquiesce to something that was very ingrained in my psyche: the need to play it safe and not disrupt and question a system of education that was oppressive and rooted in hegemony. I knew why this was happening: it was because of my own fear of failure and of not living up to some unattainable self-imposed image of myself as a doctoral student. Even within a doctoral program that encourages free expression and growth, I found myself at odds with myself, and my advisor.

I began journaling my thoughts of frustration, fear, loneliness, and pain in preparation for this monumental task. Although I enjoyed most of my coursework, I often wondered numerous times, why, why did I need a "PhD"? What does that even mean? The abstract nature of CDA provided multiple ways I could approach this topic. CDA provided me the intellectual freedom and intellectual license to pursue what would be helpful to me while I engaged this project. However, elements of wanting to be told how and what to do continued to rise within my psyche and therefore, I kept blocking myself. I knew I wanted to write about survival, the intricacies of "making it," and being successful—particularly given the multiple roles and responsibilities that I negotiated on a daily basis. While dealing with my multiple positionalities and identities, I often wanted to pick up a book or (better yet) a map to help me get through this thing called life. In fact, the times that I thought I was living, I was only existing and persevering.

While overcoming the obstacles and challenges of my existence, I knew deep down the lessons that I was learning needed to be handed down—handed down to other women who shared the common bond of womanhood. Ultimately, I needed to leave a roadmap for my own daughters. The irony in this process struck me on my head constantly. I was being told to trust my intuition, my gut, but often would not do this for fear of not being scholarly. I finally did trust my gut, which is often the way I have figured out a lot of things.

My Real Journey Begins

I chose books I had read before and authors that "spoke" to me. By that I mean, when I had read the works of Lorde, hooks, and Hill Collins previously, something deep inside me finally came back to life. I felt the yearnings of the souls of my ancestors rekindling the spirit of my soul. I realized if I were to gain freedom through this process, I would have to find it in bits and pieces, much like the slaves traveled north to their emancipation. This freedom was not found in a grand fashion, but in the collected bits and pieces of their inner strength. Mostly, I would have to find it inside. The first reading of the text had been done for classroom research or in preparation for scholarly conferences. This time, I reread all the texts by stopping and reflecting on words, phrases, sentences, and thoughts that gave me pause. I underlined them all— the words that served as kindling to the fire within my being. If I was so inclined, I made additional notations in the margins of the texts. I read a chapter at a time, and when the chapter was complete I pulled out my red journal—my keeper of the flames. It is a personal journal that I bought years ago in anticipation of this process at the heed of one of my professors, who said "write down everything—use it for your book."

I began my journey toward freedom with my red journal and my favorite fine-point black pen. I went back through the chapters of all the selected works from "my three women" and hand wrote the quotes that spoke like thunder and the ones that whispered ever so lightly to me. I knew this process would be crucial for several reasons. In order to examine the intertextuality of the selected texts, I had to know them backward and forward. Scribing also gave me an opportunity to notice the finer details of each author's writing. This process also provided the opportunity to notice what words they emphasized, when they chose to capitalize words (White, Black, etc.). And, finally, scribing allowed their words to flow between my mind and my heart. A connection was made as I wrote their very quotes. The words naturally flowed from my fingers to the tip of my favorite fine-point black pen. It was then that I realized that I began to own a piece of it—my book and the lived experiences of their texts. In between the quotes, I wrote my thoughts, experiences, and feelings that awakened by the very act of writing.

The process was a long and arduous one. Sometimes it took three hours to document two pages, sometimes after an hour, I had only one line. I repeated this process until I reached saturation in reading and had completed at the minimum the two texts. Next, I went through the journal and typed the quotes into a word document, again stopping to pause and reflect on the uniqueness of each statement or how it fit within the author's overarching theme. Did their themes "speak" to each other? How would I interpret those themes? Throughout this process it was like I had my grandmother's wisdom once again at my disposal, only this time she was able to give me hints on how to survive the often-parasitic environment of academia. I conducted a secondary and textual analysis of the following works: *Sister Outsider* (2007), by Audre Lorde and *Teaching to Transgress* (1994) by bell hooks. Because it serves as the foundation to Black feminist scholarship, I utilized *Black Feminist Thought* (1990, 2009) by Patricia Hill Collins as the central Black feminist epistemological framework. Although there are many sources of written discourse data (correspondence, publications, and unpublished), I focused primarily on publications (books) that assisted me in understanding the authors' personal and professional journeys.

Utilizing an interdiscursive analysis, which sees texts in terms of the different discourses, genres, and styles that draw upon one another and articulate together, the books were analyzed for how they have interacted with each other to create social practice, how they have influenced the standpoint of Black women, and how their works will influence the future standpoint of Black women. In addition, I considered the intertextuality of the texts, which refers to how texts draw upon, incorporate, (re)contextualize, and dialogue with other texts. This allows us to continue to recognize texts as social events, a way people can act and interact with each other and the world. This position brings to mind issues of agency and identity politics that may need to be explored.

According to Wood and Kroger (2000), patterns "involve essentially the recognition of relationships between features of discourse: within or across participants, within or across sections, within or across occasions, and so on" (117). I examined the writings of Lorde and hooks, looking for patterns in their intertextuality that may address the following questions:

- Is there an identifiable trigger for each woman when her writing becomes noticeably counterhegemonic?
- What role do words and language play for each author?
- What was the impact of the author's personal, professional, and political development on their interpersonal relationships?
- Was the author "successful" in navigating hegemonic institutions of domination?
- Were strategies for survival passed on, and how?
- How do the texts "talk" to each other? How do they "talk" to me?
- What social movements/actions have these texts created?

The above questions acted as a guide; however, I was aware that additional patterns might emerge.

In addition, part of my analysis explored "What is valid knowledge at a certain place and certain time? How does this knowledge arise, and how is it passed on? What functions does it have for constituting subjects? What consequences does it have for the overall shaping and development of society?" (Wodak and Meyer 2009, 34). This perspective fit nicely with my desire to investigate how Black women have created different ways of knowing and being in the world, how that knowledge has been validated, and how Black women have attempted to pass this information on.

This CDA may lead to the future development of a template. This template will serve as a guide for Black feminist scholars who are striving to survive and transform hegemonic institutions of domination. This template may allow emerging Black feminist scholars to see a collective pattern of psychosocial development and provide basic information on how they may begin the process of self-preservation and survival. This pattern of growth and empowerment will, of course, be unique to each woman; however, having a skeletal understanding of what the process may be in navigating the academy is crucial. It will allow for an earlier period of "normalizing" for emerging Black feminist scholars who will understand that pieces of their personal struggle have long been understood by a collective group.

Examining feelings of belonging, coping, and survival strategies for women of color who have been labeled as the "other," is really what I have been doing my whole life. I attempted at first, through one of my comprehensive questions to approach this need of belonging from a psychological perspective. I engaged one the questions from this perspective because of my counselor education training and background. But, as Lorde (2007) wrote in a letter, "I doubt that your (psych) training can have prepared you to explore the tangle of need, fear, distrust, despair and hope which operates between us, and certainly not to the depth necessary" (162). But this inquiry project has pushed me to examine this term in a broader arena as well. It has forced me to stop, step back, and reflect.

My Youth

My feelings of alienation and being "different" started as a young child. I started as a young child trying to make myself invisible, and I would literally think that if I thought I wasn't there, others could not see me. As a child, I was simultaneously praised and shunned for my light skin, big eyes, and "good hair." Often I was told that I was a beautiful child, but it always made me feel uncomfortable. This surface attention based on the Eurocentric concept of beauty denied the other pieces of who I was. People were constantly surprised that I was smart or humorous or competent, period. I finally stopped growing just shy of six feet tall and officially became an anomaly in my family. I rarely saw my paternal cousins, whom I did resemble, and it was not until 2008 at a reunion for that side of the family, I was able take a picture with them and it hit me—I look just like them.

My Schooling Experience

From this home life I added a school history that involved attending ten schools in thirteen years. I had a salad-bowl educational experience, which included Montessori, private, public, and magnet. The feeling of being different continued, magnified, grew, and festered often based on the multiple educational communities in which I participated. I received very visceral responses from people. Most were impressed and thrilled with my light skin, or they would look at me as if I am responsible for my own shading. Either way, it was very uncomfortable. In fourth grade, I attended a Montessori school in Philadelphia and in fifth and sixth grades I attended private schools. This was the beginning of feeling that same sense of "othering" from outside the community. My token status allowed me in to certain places and gave me a glimpse of cultural capital but only if I behaved. That meant answering questions about hair, sweet potato pie, and so on, or fitting in. Being quiet or silent was the key. It also meant I had to dress the part. Oxford shirts, khaki pants, penny loafers or boat shoes—the "preppy look" was always the outfit of choice.

During high school, I attended the prestigious Philadelphia High School for Girls (GHS), I began to feel the beginning of my fight with Black women. The group that looked like me, so I thought, reminded that

I didn't look like them. They also continued to remind me that I did not talk like them, act like them, or have anything in common with them. In order to survive and negotiate the oppression, I flew under the radar; hiding from them and hiding from myself. GHS was challenging; however, I still managed to graduate Summa Cum Laude.

I was accepted to Penn State, University Park campus, in the fall of 1985. I left for college on my eighteenth birthday. In retrospect I can see what a baby I was, almost a kid being sent off to war....but that's not how it was presented. I rode to college with my best friend and her parents. They picked me up from my grandmother's house and off I went. I started a new chapter of my life that continued to remind me that difference mattered, but it did not have to be in a negative way. That we could use and embrace difference. As Lorde (2007) stated, "in our work and in our living, we must recognize that difference is a reason for celebration and growth, rather than a reason for destruction" (35).

Approximately twelve hundred students out of thirty thousand on the "main" (University Park) campus were Black. I managed to be one of them. Once again thrust into an area where I had to learn the rules, the coping strategies, how to survive. Not just mentally, which was already tough—I had no idea what credits were, how they worked, how to add or drop classes, nothing. I was in the middle of Pennsylvania, a State which at the time had more hate groups than North

Carolina. And it was me, and my best friend from high school. We roomed together, and she saved me that year. She was my sister-friend. I wouldn't have made it without her. And even with the person I was most close to there were secrets. She had a daughter when she was fourteen and passed her off as her sister. So her first year at Penn State was rough because she missed her, she longed for her. I could see in her eyes that something was wrong, but it wasn't until we had lived together in a tiny room for six months that she trusted me enough to tell me her secret. Her fear kept her from living for that first year. And she didn't return for our sophomore year.

I continued to struggle through Penn State, becoming heavily involved in the Black Caucus and getting a work-study position at the Paul Robeson Cultural Center (PRCC). These two things allowed me to reduce my defenses, reload, and recharge for the daily fight—why is your perm different? What is pink lotion? Why do you wash your hair once a week? One of my roommates even asked me, challenged me, on the validity of the extra muscle theory in Black athletes (runners in particular) because all the Black runners beat her when she was in high school. They would've beaten me too. Could it be that they were just better runners?

My involvement during that sophomore year got me arrested. I found a community, and we decided that we were not going to allow the university to continue to ignore our needs. We protested, we marched, we organized, we sat-in. It was the sit-in at the telecommunications building that led to our arrest. The building was strategically selected with help from a Black faculty member as a good location because of the ground level windows (to get food in and people out if necessary) and lots of restrooms. In addition it was the "hub" of Penn State. That takeover resulted in the National Guard being called in. We were arrested (charges later were dropped) and talks resumed. The result of our action brought about change—a position was created at the upper administration level devoted to "underrepresented" groups. We selected the first hire. It never occurred to me that I could be kicked out of school; I was either passionate or stupid or passionately stupid. But it was another pivotal opportunity for me to recognize that whether or not they want to see or hear me—I will be seen and will be heard.

The summer of my junior year I got pregnant and also got kicked out of school for lack of satisfactory academic progress (too much protesting?). There I was, no place to go in Philly…no place to go in State College. One of the Black female staff members at the PRCC took me in until I could get a part-time job (waitressing at the Country Club and as a cashier at the downtown store owned by a country club member). A Black woman saved me; she knew what I needed even when I couldn't articulate it.

I never went "home" (to Philly) during that pregnancy, I stayed in State College, ignored the stares and ignorant questions and whispers and thought to myself, "How many of you have been in this situation but have chosen abortion? Why is *my* path the wrong one? Why shouldn't I be here? Why can't this work? It can. It will." More than one person just blatantly asked me how I was going to manage this. I didn't know how, but I knew I had to. The community rallied around me, and my daughter was born in Centre County. I named her "Imani," Kiswahili meaning "faith." There was only me and my future husband at her delivery. No mom, no dad, no aunts. Just us, Medicaid, WIC, and my "mother-wit." I drove her to Philly when she was three weeks old so everyone could meet her. I was twenty-one, and now I was grown.

I was readmitted to Penn State and determined to finish school with this baby, but I had no plans and no money and no transportation. Once again community rallied, and a Black basketball coach's wife introduced me to a Black football coach's wife who wanted to watch a little baby as her youngest was now five. Perfect! She charged me only what I could afford and watched Imani while I was in class *only*. It wasn't the ideal situation, but it worked.

I lived with my sister friends, and the three of us rallied around this baby. I stepped back from sit-ins and instead shifted my activism toward systemic change. My grumblings over Penn State's childcare situation led to my appointment on the Commission for Women and the Child Care Advisory Board at Penn State. I was a single Black mother in a college town receiving stares when I bought our food with food stamps, used our WIC vouchers and paid for her medicine with her Medicaid. People knew she was a basketball player's daughter, and some of the boosters would see us and look. The stares bore holes in me, which I filled with angry resolve. I graduated from undergraduate school and applied, with the encouragement of a Black faculty member I knew, to graduate school. Based on my undergraduate struggles, I didn't think I could do it. I was accepted, took the GRE, and completed the program with ease. I asked for and was granted a paid internship for the spring semester until Grad school started. This was unheard of at Penn State, a paid internship on campus. But the VP for student services was a Black man, and as the Patti Labelle song goes sometimes "beauty buys what a child gets for free." He helped me out.

My first appointment came as Director of Multicultural Affairs at a small private university in small Pennsylvania town. *Oppression and Isolation Personified*. I married (at Penn State with the reception at the Paul Robeson Cultural Center) during the blizzard of 1993, in thirty-three-and-a-half inches of snow. I had another daughter and named her Nia (Kiswahili meaning purpose). Part of her purpose is to always be a companion for her sister. After my husband completed his MBA program at PSU, we moved to Arizona where I started a PhD program in Counseling Psychology. Two children, a husband working at JC Penney and a graduate student equals hard times once again. We rented a town house with no furniture but a bed and plastic table for the kids to eat and felt immediately that we didn't fit. No one else in that complex had an MBA or was a doctoral student. *But once again I learned that in my isolation comes creation.* I learned how to survive again. This time I even went to the food bank several times to feed us. And I remember the loathing I had for the only other Black woman in the program, older than me, who wasn't struggling. *I resented her, and she didn't know why. I didn't know why.* I stared at my class issues straight on. It didn't matter what credentials we had: we were poor; we had a common denominator with our neighbors. But we didn't talk like them, so they thought we were "beyond" them. Once again in the middle: too poor to hang out with the rich, and too rich to be poor. *Or so they wanted us to believe.*

We left Arizona and moved to Colorado to begin to follow my husband's career and begin our path toward upward (or uppity) mobility. I had another child, this time a son. We named him Nathan, meaning a gift from God. While in Colorado, I worked with the several nonprofit organizations founded to "create change" and "help those in poverty"; but no one working at those organizations was in need. I was the token representative they needed to make themselves feel all right. Organizations for change in a town that only pretended to embrace diversity. The median cost of a starter home was around $250,000. The illusion of diversity was more like it. To battle what children of color being raised in Boulder might experience, I worked with a nonprofit that gathered us together two times a month, took field trips, put on plays and performances, and even took a trip to South Africa. The organization supported many children during my five years with them, sadly, however, three children still lost their paths and committed suicide. One wrote a traveling journey that touches the heartbeat of this inquiry project with his isolation and alienation.

Our move to North Carolina allowed me to enter a program that gave me the freedom to research my experiences and see that I have come full circle. This program liberated me, and this research helped me reclaim the voice I tried to silence so I could desperately fit into suburbia—pampered chef, tastefully simple, soirees, tennis, golf, piano recitals, swim team, and horseback riding—I wanted it all, I wanted my kids to be "normal." I know now there is no normal...just the "mythical norm" we get sucked into believing is real.

This same type of obedience was implied as I attended a recent summer institute for doctoral students. I was so excited about the opportunity to engage in "scholarly discourse." But I found that there too, I was expected to recognize the pecking order of privilege—*race*. Then whatever else you want to throw in. Oh wait, but not lesbians and gays. They don't exist. I spoke up when I was asked to privilege various pieces of me over other pieces and was almost eaten alive by my "brothers." Afterward, every young woman in attendance (most of the attendees were under thirty years old) approached me and said "I was thinking the same thing," but no one said anything. I doubted myself in that dorm room that night for a long time, fighting myself, using my energy against myself, because *I knew* I was correct. Why did it bother me so? Why was I so afraid to become an anathema? And I did. For the rest of that institute several "brothers" wouldn't speak to me. I looked around the room with my "brothers" and "sisters," and I am still alone. A pivotal point for me in writing this book, as I found my voice that weekend and realized that it comes, sometimes with isolation and alienation. I forgot. But you cannot forget. It is not a luxury of the Black woman.

And my journey continues, I fight at this HBCU. I fight for me, and I fight for you. I am trying to educate, liberate these students. On a campus full of fear, hatred, and oppression I try to push against the margin and use it. Own it. Claim it. I cringe as I witness an education of oppression and victimization that allows the headlines of the local newspaper to scream "Big Changes at a local HBCU," but those changes are about how hard the cheerleaders shake their asses. And the more the better. The higher the heels the better. And no one challenges that our students dress as if they are ready for battle and their gear is make up, high heels, and oppression.

I have lived in a large urban cities and rural areas, populated with both progressive and conservative people as part of my journey. My lens continued to change with my marriage and the birth of each child. Most recently my lens has been shifted by my socioeconomic status and my geographical isolation, as I do not live near any family or close friends. The isolation is exacerbated by the neighborhood in which we live, which is 4 percent Black and has a median income of $77,510 for a household. My hobbies, such as tennis, swimming, and triathlons, and educational pursuits continue to put me in places in which I am often the only Black. This type of isolation continues to fuel my passion for wanting to investigate how other Black women have navigated their psychological tight spaces amid increasing shifting geographical and economic conditions. How have they found their voice and dealt with their alienation and isolation. How will I? So again, ultimately this piece is about me, Shawn _Arango_ Ricks. I no longer fear how this will be received, who I will offend, and how many times I must use the word "hegemonic" to prove my intelligence. To whom? I know many words, but the only useful ones will be those that can cross barriers and build bridges back to those I started to leave behind.

FIVE

LORDE, HOOKS,
AND THEIR BLACK FEMINIST RHETORIC(S)

It is sometimes both the curse and the blessing of the
poet to perceive without yet being able to order those
perceptions and that is another name for chaos. But it is
out of chaos that new worlds are born. I look forward to
our meeting eye to eye.

—*Audre Lorde*

The distinguishing features and core themes of Black feminist thought provide the foundation necessary to explore the role of bell hooks and Audre Lorde for today's Black women as they navigate their psychological tight spaces. Lorde and hooks have been identified because they most closely align with my experiences as they have written extensively about their psychological tight spaces. Although they represent a miniscule proportion of African American women who navigate the hostile terrains of hegemonic institutions on a daily basis, the interconnectedness of their oppressions once again demonstrates the collective consciousness of Black women. Each scholar has documented her unique perspective on dealing with the marginality and domination throughout multiple areas of their lives.

Audre Lorde: *The Master's Tools*

Audre Lorde was selected, in part, for her work on the "many layers of selfhood" as well as the emancipatory nature of her writing. In 1979, Audre Lorde, a Black feminist educator/scholar, lesbian/queer, poet, challenged the "lily white halls" of academia by demanding that her White feminist colleagues deconstruct and take stock in the type of work they engaged. In a fifteen-minute address to a largely White, entitled and privileged feminist audience at the Second Sex Conference in New York, Lorde launched a ballistic literary missile of enigmatic proportions: she challenged academic feminists to destroy the oppressive structures of the academy and create anew. The address, "The Master's Tools Will Never Dismantle the Master's House," was a quantum leap for feminist activism. More than thirty years later, many academic feminists are still at a crossroads regarding, "this old house." Her work also explores issues of belonging and reconciliation of self throughout her numerous books and poems, touching on many important components of who I am, and who I have yet to become. She has made me realize the importance of my own self-empowerment and preservation as I navigate my psychological tight spaces.

The following passage illustrates this point well:

> Acting like an insider and feeling like the outsider, preserving our own self-rejection as Black women at the same time as we're getting over— we think. And political work will not save our souls, no matter how correct and necessary that work is. Yet it is true that without political work we cannot hope to survive long enough to effect any change. And self-empowerment is the most deeply political work there is, and the most difficult. (Lorde 2007, 170)

Lorde's work is important because it integrates all the loose ends of hooks and Hill Collins and fuses them to my yet unformed thoughts. She discusses issues surrounding mothering, anger, marginalization, and relationships, in a way that compels me to learn more. Her insights on living, loving and learning, provide more information for me on ways to survive in parasitic environments. Her insights provide information I did not hear or learn as a child and have not been exposed to yet as an adult. Certainly this can provide for me a new way of being, inclusive of all my complex parts and aware of the complex skills necessary to navigate institutions of domination without sacrificing any part of myself.

Reading Lorde and hooks was a powerful experience for me in unique and different ways. I don't purport to be an expert on all aspects of the lives of either woman, just an expert on the pieces of both of them that I needed to embrace. Where Lorde screamed at me through her text with an urgency and intensity in which a mother screams at a child who is in danger; hooks whispered to me with a grandmotherly comfort, reminding me to hold on. Hold on.

I found in the work of Lorde the information I needed to begin healing and connecting all the fragmented pieces of my selves. In the initial conceptualization of this book, I spoke of and researched the concept of multiple identities. Lorde, using different terminology, touches on this in her work and validates what I could not name, but *knew* was there. I use her work as the framework for healing, in the broadest definition possible. That is the beauty of discourse; we interact with it and create social spaces based on these interactions. And every interaction with a text can be different, for every time we read it we are a different person.

hooks provided me the information I needed to continue in my current role as a professor and program coordinator of a large undergraduate program at a HBCU. The work has been overwhelming. For the first time in my teaching career (which started at Penn State almost twenty years ago), I feel done—"bone weary," as she calls it. Reading her work, believing it would liberate me from my personal demons, she continued instead to whisper to me about the role and need of education as a liberatory practice. And while doing that, she taught me one of the golden rules of working with qualitative data: you must be open to change.

In Lorde's work I found an overarching theme of survival, physical and psychological, threaded throughout each piece of work I read, and all the subthemes. She demands from herself, that in order to strive for survival, she must define what survival means to her. She states that "survival is the ability to encompass difference, to encompass change without destruction" (Lorde 2007, 75). I explore her definition of this term, and what it means to her by interrogating the subthemes of self-definition, self-love, sisterhood, adaptability, voice, power, and language. As Lorde (2007) notes, "we are powerful because we have survived, and that is what it is all about—*survival and growth*" (139, emphasis added).

Lorde's battle with cancer had an immense impact on her view of survival—she was in a fight for her life, yet she was able to recognize during her bouts with cancer—that ultimately we are all in a fight for our lives. She writes: "Racism. Cancer. In both cases, to win the aggressor must conquer but the resisters need only survive. How do I define that survival and on whose terms?" (Lorde 2007, 132). Lorde recognizes early on that she will have to decide for herself what survival will look like, incorporating a subtheme to be explored later in more detail—the importance of self-definition.

To fully explicate and tease out Lorde's themes, I have written a fictional dialogue, as if I were sitting across the kitchen table from her. This dialogue is a combination of my interpretation of how Audre Lorde would answer my questions and direct quotes. The information is gathered primarily from *Sister Outsider* (2007) and *I Am Your Sister: Collected and Unpublished Writings of Audre Lorde* (2009). To remain true to the organic nature of this dialogue, there are no citations throughout.

Breaking Bread with Audre

> SR: Thank you very much for giving so much information via your work. Historical coping tools used by Black women continue to shift, and I am searching for ways to continue to survive both inside and outside of the academy. What can you share with me about survival?

> Lorde: "The first and most vital lesson [is] that we were never meant to survive. Not as human beings."

> SR: What do you mean by that?

> Lorde: It is important to recognize that "survival," the term, can be viewed as a tool. If you think you're surviving, you are just getting by. Yes, you may be alive, but in what form? Do you not want to thrive? Will you be brain-dead, your ideas co-opted and used against yourself and our people? Ultimately, you need to decide what survival means to you. For me it "is the ability to encompass difference, to encompass change without destruction."

SR: That's right, I guess I never really thought about it, but your work really awakened something inside of me that I think was destroyed—was dead. Survival is complex, and I believe there were parts of myself that I had allowed to die. I was so busy trying to make sure I knew all the rules of the game; I drifted away from some core pieces of me.

Lorde: It is important that you do know the game, "for in order to survive, those of us for whom oppression is as American as apple pie have always had to be watchers, to become familiar with the language and manners of the oppressor, even sometimes adopting them for some illusion of protection." Given what you've told me about your upbringing, time in private schools and hostile college environment, you've had to learn how to be a little bit like them. Not to protect only you but also your children. Also your children.

SR: That's right, I had my first child as a single parent in college, and I think I was afraid for her. I've always been afraid for all of them and stuck with my choices. Raise them in the suburbs or in the "hood." I hate that I have to make a call on that. Hate it.

Lorde: Being a Black mother is hard, and it's your responsibility to teach your children how to survive. "And survival is the greatest gift of love. Sometimes, for Black mothers it is the only gift possible, and tenderness gets lost."

SR: Yes, I know. The kids think I'm harsh sometimes, and they often ask me why I am so angry. You know, I tell them, I don't know any other way to be!

Lorde: As parents, we teach our children continuously, through our words, our actions, and our nonactions. "My mother taught me to survive from a very early age by her own example. Her silence also taught me isolation fury, mistrust, self-rejection, and sadness. My survival lay in learning how to use weapons she gave me, also, to fight against those things within myself, unnamed." A lot my writing has become healing as a result, and as I note in my essay, "Poetry is not a luxury." When you are hurt, you need to find a way to heal. Perhaps we are also mourning the loss of our childhood and the loss of mothering, which is a luxury that Black parents just can't give sometimes, and that we may no longer be able to receive.

SR: I think you may be onto something there. Mourning the loss of a mother is big for me. I haven't lived near my family since for over twenty-five years, I had to use your advice and "learn to mother" myself. But, even in doing so, I still felt angry....

Lorde: And that's fine, feel anger, feel anything...you have to allow yourself time for the mourning, the anger, your losses. As Black women we must remember that "the piece we paid for learning survival was our childhood. We were never allowed to be children. It is the right of children to be able to play at living for a little while, but for a Black child, every act can have deadly serious consequences, and for a Black girl child, even more so. You've not been allowed to be a child, and you don't have a mother anymore. So acknowledge, embrace, own your feelings...and don't separate them from your mind...Now when males or patriarchal thinkers (whether male or female) reject that combination, then we're truncated. Rationality is not unnecessary. It serves to get from this place to that place. But if you don't honor those places, then the road is meaningless. Too often, that's what happens with the worship of rationality and that circular, academic, analytic thinking. But ultimately, I don't see feel/think as a dichotomy. I see them as a choice of ways and combinations.

SR: Be careful of the "mind/body" dichotomy hooks refers to?

Lorde: Yes, it's better to be angry than to not feel anything at all. You see, feeling is key to your liberation. "The white fathers told us: I think, therefore I am. The Black mother within each of us—the poet—whispers in our dreams: I feel, therefore I can be free." Your freedom, all of our freedom, is wrapped up in feeling...connecting and conquering the dark places within our souls we've been too afraid to touch. Anger being one of them.

SR: There's such a negative stereotype on anger, and so many labels on Black women as angry. From a counseling perspective, I love teaching about anger, mostly because it is often referred to as a secondary emotion. The students immediately disagree, and then we get to the process of learning...showing them how to connect the dots! Taking examples of when they were "angry" and having them examine them to find out the underlying emotion—pain, frustration, hurt, jealousy. There's always an underlying emotion.

Lorde: Anger does get a bad rap, but it shouldn't. Anger is fine; it's hate that is dangerous. And to me there is a difference. To me "anger [is] a passion of displeasure that may be excessive or misplaced but not necessarily harmful. Hatred [is] an emotional habit or attitude of mind in which aversion is coupled with ill will. Anger, used, does not destroy. Hate does."

SR: I think I needed to hear that. I notice you use the word "passion" when describing anger.

Lorde: Yes, it is a "passion of displeasure"—you feel it deeply, passionately. But it still doesn't destroy you, if you use it.

SR: I think I've left a lot of anger floating around in me, unused. Going, with my secondary emotion theory, I would have to say that the bulk of my anger is based on hurt—both personal and systemic.

Lorde: "It is easier to be angry than to hurt. Anger is what I do best. It is easier to be furious than to be yearning." And, over time and through my reading of the *I Ching*, I realized that even those things I was angry about—little girls dying, Black boys failing, Black women hating each other—that I had little control over, I needed to recognize and withdraw. And anger is not unique to you! "Women of Color in america have grown up within a symphony of anger, at being silenced, at being unchosen, at knowing that when we survive, it is in spite of a world that takes for granted our lack of humanness and which hates our very existence outside of its service. And I say symphony rather than cacophony because we have had to learn to orchestrate these furies so that they do not tear us apart. We have had to learn to move through them and use them for strength and force and insight within our daily lives. Those of us who did not learn this difficult lesson did not survive. And part of my anger is always in libation for my fallen sisters."

SR: So I need to find out how to use my anger, all my emotions really, for strength within my daily life?

Lorde: Yes, and one of the first steps will be to love yourself. Attack the "passion of displeasure" with the passion of love. Self-love will mean facing all your feelings, owning them, using them, defining yourself, embracing your sisters, finding your voice, and claiming your power. Understanding the oppression you've internalized and swallowed and spit it back up. And reconcile the contradictions that are within you, that are within all of us. Self-love is critical to our survival.

SR: Yes, those are all pieces I feel I need help in and areas in which I feel our ancestors recognized we needed to work on. When you look at the early work of slave women, writers of the Harlem Renaissance, calls for action, and so on, there was this urgency for change for action—even though not perfect, which is missing now. Now there seems to be a complacency.

Lorde: It is urgent that we love ourselves. "We have to love ourselves and we [Black people] have to love every piece of our brothers and sisters."

SR: That's critical, you're right. I have to love myself. And I have to love my brothers and sisters.

Lorde: "every piece."

SR: Every piece?

Lorde: Yes, one of the downfalls of the Black community has been homophobia. We can't pick and choose which parts of people we'll love.

SR: I agree. When I was in college, I was...um...different. I had a different perspective on a lot of things. I wore two buttons on my book bag all through college. One from Brother Malcolm X stating "by any means necessary," and a button of your quote "Silence is the voice of complicity." I always felt that if someone will talk about one group with me in the room, they'll talk about Blacks, women, Latinos, etc....whatever group is their target du jour. I had an interesting experience this summer regarding a choice to be silent or to speak up. I participated in the National Council for Black Studies Summer Institute for PhD students. I was thrilled to be selected and excited about what I knew would be an intellectually stimulating and enriching think tank.

Lorde: That sounds like a great opportunity.

SR: For the most part it was, but as we discuss the need for solidarity and self-love, I will share two disappointing pieces.

Lorde: OK.

SR: The first incident happened when I challenged a "brother" on gay-bashing as he discussed the Harlem Renaissance. This "gentleman" was another institute participant, and, well, over the top. He wanted to be the alpha dog, if you know what I mean. But I was one of the older participants, with a lot of lived experience to share. When I challenged him, he barked back that there were no gays during the Harlem Renaissance, and it didn't matter either way. Then one of the male facilitators says "We're Black first"...and the men rally around this. Including Maulana Karenga (who created Kwanzaa), who was there to facilitate a session later that afternoon.

Lorde: So, in an environment you thought would be supportive of every piece of who you are, you felt attacked.

SR: Yes, it's like you can never let your guard down—never. Anyway, I resisted. I challenged. I said to the group that I could not privilege one piece of myself over another piece. And, even if I could, I wouldn't. The room was silent. There were no women facilitators there to support me (there were only two on the agenda; one had to leave after she presented and one wasn't there yet). The other young women in the room were silent. But afterward one by one they sought me out to say that they agreed. And the young man, he didn't speak or look at me for the rest of the conference.

Lorde: That's exactly what I mean. "There is always someone asking you to underline one piece of yourself—whether it's Black, woman, mother, dyke, teacher, etc.—because that's the piece that they need to key in to. They want to dismiss everything else. But once you do that, then you've lost, because then you become acquired or bought by that particular essence of yourself and you've denied yourself all of the energy that it takes to keep all those others in jail. Only by learning to live in harmony with your contradictions can you keep it all afloat."

SR: That's how I felt exactly, I felt dismissed. And angry! (smile). But I persevered. I wanted to leave; I wanted to run and hide. I questioned myself, you know, no one else was speaking. The next day, a female facilitator led a discussion on Black women's literature, in particular the piece *The Color Purple*. As her allotted time was about to expire, Karenga again spoke up, took over really. He shared his sense of disappointment with Alice

112

Walker for not showing more positive Black males in her novel. His five-minute diatribe on this took us right to the lunch hour. Our afternoon session would be led by a man. Again. Something deep within me stirred, and I think I felt the beginnings of the connection you speak of (self-love plus voice plus feeling equals power). Somehow, I felt powerful enough to approach him, someone I once idolized, and challenge him on that statement. But more than that, I raised the irony that the last voice we heard from during the small section we (Black women) had was a BLACK MALE...talking about how bad a Black woman has treated them.

Lorde: Yes, you see once you love yourself enough, find your voice, acknowledge the "Back mother" within you...you have begun to reclaim your power!

SR: Yea, it was surreal. It was great. Over lunch I noticed the male elders who run NCBS discussing the implications of homophobia, so that was cool. You know, to plant a seed and start discussion. And, as a result of my other observation, we spent an additional hour after lunch allowing my sister to finish up her presentation. It was phenomenal. I felt energized, renewed. And not how I thought I would be.

Lorde: We need those experiences. We need to stand up for and defend our "multiplicities of self." "As a Black lesbian feminist comfortable with the many different ingredients of my identity, and a woman committed to racial and sexual freedom from oppression, I find I am constantly being encouraged to pluck out some one aspect of myself and present this as a meaningful whole, eclipsing or denying the other parts of self. But this is a destructive and fragmenting way to live. My fullest concentration of energy is available to me only when I integrate all the parts of who I am, openly, allowing power from particular sources of my living to flow back and forth freely through all my different selves, without the restrictions of an externally imposed definition."

SR: Yes, your concept of "multiplicities of selves" really resonates within me. I tried to approach this in an earlier paper I wrote, but I used the term "identity" and approached it from a counseling perspective. But you have captured what I was trying to say. That when people force me to choose, interact with only the piece of me they desire...then I begin to feel trapped by those "externally imposed definitions" and that's how I developed the phrase "psychological tight spaces."

Lorde: "With respect to myself specifically, I feel that not to be open about any of the different 'people' within my identity, particularly the 'mes' who are challenged by a status quo, is to invite myself and other women, by my example to live a lie. In other words, I would be giving in to a myth of sameness which I think can destroy us." So, it's kind of interesting that you wore that button all throughout college "Silence is the voice of complicity." If I am silent about who I am or don't speak up in defense of others (even if it's other pieces of me!)...I am complicit.

SR: Yes, I finally got that. I still have the button. It's on a singing frog in my office. It reminds me daily not to leave my voice at the door when I come to work! Now that I work at a HBCU in the south, I am constantly reminded that Black heterosexual male privilege rules. There is a belief in the hierarchy of oppression on this campus and in many HBCUs.

Lorde: It is important that we work at abolishing "horizontal hostility." Although "the tactic of encouraging horizontal hostility to becloud more pressing issues of oppression is by no means new, nor limited to relations between women. The same tactic is used to encourage separation between Black women and Black men. In discussions around the hiring and firing of Black faculty at universities, the charge is frequently heard that Black women are more easily hired than are Black men. For this reason, Black women's promotion and tenure are not considered important since they are only taking jobs away from Black men."

SR: Yes, I see that working at a HBCU comes with a unique set of problems, the crabs in a barrel syndrome, if you will. There is very little room for difference at a HBCU. You Black. Just be Black.

Lorde: Yes, it's true that there are lots of similarities shared among people who share a cultural background; however, "in order to work together we [Black people]do not have to become a mix of indistinguishable particles resembling a vat of homogenized chocolate milk."

SR: I think that's the expectation, and I walk around that campus feeling like an outsider as well. Needing, wanting more from the others on campus—students, faculty, and staff. The campus is without feeling, and in such an environment the pursuit of liberation can be difficult. I am on a campus where, for the most part, feminism is still a dirty word and women are invisible. The other Black women on campus have not formed a community that I am aware of, and as eagerly as I search for survival tools for life, I am also aware that if I am going to maintain longevity in the academy I will also need to develop survival skills, some may be the same, some may be different.

Lorde: In academia, and in life, "the failure…to recognize differences as a crucial strength is a failure to reach beyond the first patriarchal lesson. In our world, divide and conquer must become define and empower."

SR: And the "define and empower" must be for all! Black men and women, straight and gay, white women, all.

Lorde: Ultimately, yes. "Within the interdependence of mutual (nondominant) differences lies that security which enables us to descend into the chaos of knowledge and return with true visions of our future, along with the concomitant power to effect those changes which can bring that future into being. Difference is that raw and powerful connection from which our personal power is forged."

SR: Personal power through difference and connection. No matter what, we need each other ultimately. I guess I was hopeful that working at a HBCU would be different, that I wouldn't be invisible and that sisterhood would come. I would build and find networks. We have a lot of Black women in key positions on campus, but they still work twice as hard as the men to prove...I don't know what. And even with those supposedly visible women, I had to put in a work order to request feminine hygiene receptacles in the women's bathroom near my office. Another opportunity to use my voice! And, again, no one appreciated that they weren't there. It's terribly awkward, borderline humiliating, as a woman not to have access to dispose of feminine hygiene products. All the women I spoke to agreed that it was odd. And now I smile daily when I see that I made a small change. But you reminded me that revolution is not a one-time event. I have to keep fighting, keep speaking. But I can't seem to find that sense of female solidarity on campus that I am yearning for.

Lorde: Yes, oh my yes. I am familiar with the atmosphere of HBCUs from my time at Tougaloo. Definitely an interesting dynamic example of how deeply entrenched the oppressor can become in one's soul. And for liberation, for your survival to get back to your original question, Black women will need to "move against not only those forces which dehumanize from the outside, but also against those oppressive values which we have been forced to take into ourselves." And remember, survival is about growth and change. "As Paulo Friere shows so well in The Pedagogy of the Oppressed, the true focus of revolutionary change is never merely the oppressive situations which we seek to escape, but that piece of the oppressor which is planted deep within each of us, and which knows only the oppressors' tactics, the oppressors' relationships."

SR: Growth and change. I feel a lot of resistance around this concept. There is fear of change and growth because it's new, it's uncomfortable.

Lorde: Yes, it is uncomfortable, because "change means growth, and growth can be painful. But we sharpen self-definition by exposing the self in work and struggle together with those whom we define as different from ourselves, although sharing the same goals. For Black and white, old and young, lesbian and heterosexual women alike, this can mean new paths to our survival." But reaching across difference is so crucial; we need that community, that sisterhood. I often think about how my life would've been different if I had the opportunity to make connections with other women. I am saddened to think about how Angelian Grimke, a Black lesbian poet during the Harlem Renaissance, died alone. Isolated. I was across town struggling in isolation at Hunter College. We both thought we were alone, but we could've supported each other, helped each other, and guided each other through. "I think of what it could have meant in terms of sisterhood and survival for each one of us to have known of the other's existence for me to have her words and her wisdom, and for her to have known I needed them! It is so crucial for each one of us to know she is not alone."

SR: That's what strikes me most about your writing and the writing of bell hooks. It reminds me that I am not alone. In counseling terms we call that normalizing. People often get locked into thinking that their circumstances are totally unique to them, and no one can understand. But that's not true! Your words and your wisdom are here, through your literature, anytime I need them. That's a powerful piece of the power of language that can't be denied.

Lorde: You are right, language is powerful, and it can bring a whole community together or tear one apart! But for me "poetry is not a luxury. It is a vital necessity for our existence." It is "through poetry that we give name to those ideas which are—until the poem—nameless and formless, about to be birthed, but already felt."

SR: So, for you language holds one of the keys to my survival?

Lorde: Yes, for *our* survival. "Each one of us is here now because in one way or another we share a commitment to language and to the power of language, and to the reclaiming of that language which has been made to work against us. In the transformation of silence into language and action, it is vitally necessary for each one of us to establish or examine her function in that transformation."

SR: "The transformation of silence into language and action." This phrase reminds me of the Frierian concept of praxis hooks discusses when she talks about her work in the classroom. Also, you believe strongly in the usefulness of destroying our silences and finding our voice as a liberatory tool.

Lorde: Yes. Over time "I have come to believe over and over again that what is most important to me must be spoken, made verbal and shared, even at the risk of having it bruised or misunderstood."

SR: That is one of your more well-known quotes, but it doesn't diminish its effect, if you really read it. And you use very powerful, deliberate language when you speak and write.

Lorde: I have to. If we are to move through this process we have to recognize that silence and fear are not going to liberate us. They did not liberate our ancestors. They spoke and wrote and ran—with the risk of physical death. For me, for us, we risk a spiritual death if we don't speak. I am aware that "there are so many ways in which I'm vulnerable and cannot help but be vulnerable, I'm not going to be more vulnerable by putting weapons of silence in my enemies' hands."

SR: If I view language as a tool for liberation and survival, then I guess it makes sense that silence could be a weapon. I never really connected those dots consciously, although I think subconsciously I must have, otherwise why would I keep a college button for twenty-five years?

Lorde: Yes, and if you buy into the silence, the obedience, the docility than you become easier to manipulate. You begin to accept the "many facets of our oppression as women." And for us, for women of Color, we have to recognize that to white women we are the "other, the outsider whose experience is too alien to comprehend."

SR: Yes, "the other." I think this describes some of my feelings when I moved into the suburbs, joined tennis teams, went to preschool playdates...with moms that didn't look like me. No one ever says it. Ever. But I can feel it. I am welcome, as long as I behave. I guess sometimes I feel like the token Black family in our community!

Lorde: Be mindful that the "tokenism that is sometimes extended to us is not an invitation to own power."

SR: I thought I could belong, if I "played nice." But daily, I was swallowing things subconsciously; caught up in my world. Tricked by the plate of "equity" placed before me.

Lorde: And that's not just you. "It is easier for white women to believe the dangerous fantasy that if you are good enough, pretty enough, sweet enough, quiet enough, teach the children to behave, hate the right people, and marry the right man, then you will be allowed to coexist with patriarchy in relative peace."

SR: Yes, fifteen years I've wasted hoping to be allowed to "coexist" in "relative peace."

Lorde: No experience is ever wasted. Without that realization, without having experienced it, you could not be a witness for it. "Unless one lives and loves in the trenches it is difficult to remember that the war against dehumanization is ceaseless."

SR: Yes, I thought that I could just focus on "making it." You know, having "the dream." But I was so foolish! I don't want the dream, I want my dream. It just didn't feel right, it was starting to feel forced. Once I got everything, the dream said I needed a husband, a house, cars, cat, dog, three kids. I still felt this emptiness, this yearning to do more—fulfill **my** dream.

Lorde: You were indeed feeling trapped. "Somewhere, on the edge of consciousness, there is what I call a mythical norm, which each one of us within our hearts knows 'that is not me'...It is within this mythical norm that the trappings of power reside within this society. Those of us who stand outside that power often identify one way in which we are different and we assume that to be the primary cause of all oppression, forgetting other distortions around differences, some of which we ourselves may be practicing." It sounds like you realized you were not being true to you, and by doing so and not recognizing the ways in which you were privileged, you became part of the oppression of others.

SR: And it's a rude awakening. Although I don't think I was one hundred percent asleep; for me it was more like a coma. So, I guess it's been like a reawakening, a rebirth.

Lorde: Yes, that's fine. That's good. You, like all of us, have had to adapt. Now, you must take this experience and use it. Use all your experiences. This is "one of the most basic Black survival skills...the ability to change, to metabolize experience, good or ill, into something that is useful, lasting, effective." Now that you have had the experience, what will you *do* with it. You speak of your dream. How will you define that? How will you define you?

SR: How will I define me?

Lorde: Yes, you are in a battle for survival, but before you build your army and your community of support, you have to know your position on the battlefield. You won't know this until you know you. And if you know you, define you, and then you won't be swallowed up by other's definitions of who you should be. It's something that I had to discover, and then live by...that "if I didn't define myself for myself, I would be crunched into other people's fantasies for me and eaten alive."

SR: That's powerful.

Lorde: And, it's true! "If we do not define ourselves for ourselves, we will be defined by others—for their use and to our detriment." So, you see it's not really an option. "As Black women we have the right and responsibility to define ourselves and to seek our allies in common cause." Once you define yourself, accept yourself, love yourself, you can begin to reach across, back and through to others to build your community of support, knowing that "nothing [you] accept about [your]self can be used against [you] to diminish [you]."

SR: So self-love, self-definition is another vital component of survival?

Lorde: Yes, and using it then to help you face your fears to build alliances. You will have to learn to be "open and self-protective" at the same time?

SR: How can that be? How can I guard myself while welcoming you in to help me build the community I need?

Lorde: It will take determination and practice, but I imagine you've done this to a certain extent in your life already. "Black women who survive have a head start on learning how to be open and self-protective at the same time. One secret is to ask as many people as possible for help, depending on all of them and none of them at the same time. Some will help, others cannot. For the time being."

SR: I stopped.

Lorde: You stopped?

SR: Yes, I stopped asking for help, depending on people.

Lorde: You were hurt, afraid?

SR: Yes, both. I built a community when I raised my daughter during her early years at Penn State, and it was great. It really was.

Lorde: So you see that "without community there is no liberation, only the most vulnerable and temporary armistice between an individual and her oppression. But community must not mean a shedding of our difference, nor the pathetic pretense that those differences do not exist."

SR: Yes, I believe in the individual power that can be harnessed through community.

Lorde: What happened? Why did you stop?

SR: Well, for one, we moved away from everyone. This was before social networking. We stayed in touch, but it's not the same. What really happened was I saw how fear magnified can destroy what takes years to build. My best friend came to visit with her husband and three-year-old son. We put the boys (my son was eight at the time) to bed, and went to the store for some private time. Her husband checked on the boys, and they were out of bed, naked in the bathroom. The immediate response from both of them (out of homophobic fear) was that something was terribly wrong. Their son told them that my son told him to take his clothes off and get in bed with him. I believed it, but I know my son. He is a nurturer. It was hot. He would have problem solved and tried to comfort a younger person; then taken him to the bathroom to use it. Anyway, the pain of them leaving the next morning abruptly shook me to my core. Finally, all my worlds were colliding. We were both Black women, we were all Black...but the fear of difference...the homophobia...nullified that. Instantly.

Lorde: That's a powerful, and it seems, a painful story. Are you still in touch?

SR: We tried to talk, but I cannot do anything that doesn't feel right. I can't do it if it's not from my soul. Through this process—my book, your words—I have the strength to find my voice and write to her with my true feelings. I feel sad, but it has to be this way.

Lorde: I can hear the sadness in your voice, but I also hear fear. You do not have the luxury of being afraid to build another community or to reach out. You must do it. This is another piece that will help you reclaim your power, your survival.

SR: Yes, there is fear there. I am afraid. I must remind myself of one of my favorite quotes by you, "When I dare to be powerful, to use my strength in the service of my vision, then it becomes less and less important whether I am afraid."

Lorde: Do you dare to be powerful. It's inside you; it's inside all of us.

SR: [silence]

Lorde: Do you dare to be powerful?

SR: Yes. I resolve: *I dare to be powerful*. And I know, "to search for power within myself means I must be willing to move through being afraid to whatever lies beyond."

Lorde: "Where does our power lie and how do we school ourselves to use it in the service of what we believe?" It lies within, but you must be in touch with it. You "must be in touch with our own ancient roads in which lies deep power for each woman" and "as we come more in touch with our ancient, non-European consciousness of living as a situation to be experienced and interacted with, we learn more and more to cherish our feelings, and to respect those hidden sources of our power from where true knowledge, and therefore lasting action comes."

SR: Thanks so much for taking this journey with me. It has truly been transformative.

Lorde: You are welcome my sister, you are welcome. Remember as you continue on your personal and political journey that "there are no new ideas still waiting in the wings to save us as women, as human. There are only old and forgotten ones, new combinations extrapolations and recognitions from within ourselves—along with the renewed courage to try them out."

After the Meal

This dialogue was an unplanned cathartic experience. Not only was I unsure of what I would discover at the start of my journey, I did not know exactly how the analysis would look. I started this analysis with an idea in mind to use each theme as a subheading and explain Lorde's definition for each of them. Five minutes into the analysis, the dialogue began in my head, and I decided to allow it to flow. This was the right angle to take to explore Lorde, because it was effortless. Lorde's overarching theme of survival (physical and psychological) is accomplished through the acquisition and use of power. Reclaiming our power involves the following: voice (language, feelings), adaptability, and self-love (self-definition, multiplicities of self, sisterhood).

Power. The theme of power involves finding our voice, embracing adaptability, and self-love. Our ultimate power lies inside each of us, and always has. It lies dormant, waiting for us to recognize, own, unleash, and embrace it. What we know intuitively is often counterattacked through dominant discourses of fear that we will find ourselves within ourselves. This view of intuitive knowledge has been termed many things: the Black poet within, mother-wit, and la facultad (Anzaldúa 1987). Regardless of how we name it, its basic premise remains the same. If we are able to acknowledge, unlock, and use our feelings to connect to our inner power we will find our liberation.

There are no new ideas still waiting in the wings to save us as women, as human. There are only old and forgotten ones, new combinations, extrapolations, and recognitions *from within ourselves*—along with the renewed courage to try them out. (Lorde 2007, 38, emphasis added)

Voice. Voice involves the ability to acknowledge your feelings and address and conquer the fear that keeps us standing still. It also involves destroying the silences, slowly choking us. Lorde (2007) believes that to "suppress any truth is to give it strength beyond endurance" (58), which then places additional power in the hands of our enemies. If we begin to suppress truths and allow ourselves to be externally defined, we begin to accept and become complicit in our oppression as women. Instead of silence, Lorde (2007) challenges us by asking,

What are the tyrannies you swallow day by day and attempt to make your own, until you will sicken and die of them, still in silence? Perhaps...because I am myself—a Black woman warrior poet doing my work—come to ask you, are you doing yours. (41–42)

Silence, according to Lorde, is deadly. You may not physically die from it, but you surely will never *live* in it.

Feelings are a large theme in the work of Audre Lorde. As a Black, feminist, lesbian poet, she disconnected and reconnected with her selves and her community multiple times. All of which demanded she acknowledge her feelings. If we acknowledge our feelings then we can use them to increase our power. We have a finite amount of energy, and if we are consciously or subconsciously using it to suppress truths, we will never discover our full potential. Lorde (2007) states:

> There is a distinction I am beginning to make in my living between pain and suffering. Pain is an event, and experience that must be named, recognized and then used in some way in order for the experience to change, to be transformed into something else, strength or knowledge or action.
>
> Suffering, on the other hand, is the nightmare reliving of unscrutinized and ummetabolized pain. *When I live through pain without recognizing it, self-consciously, I rob myself of the power that can come from using the pain, the power to fuel some movement beyond it.* I condemn myself to reliving that pain over and over whenever something close triggers it. And that is suffering, a seemingly inescapable cycle. (171–172, emphasis added)

Adaptability. Whether discussing feelings, or a personal challenge, Lorde (2007) believes that "one of the most basic Black survival skills is the ability to change, to metabolize experience, good or ill, into something that is useful, lasting, effective" (135). This gift will, and has, allowed Blacks and other marginalized groups resistance domination, and create pockets of liberation.

Self-love. Discovering and using voice demands an engagement in self-love and self-definition. Several of Lorde's well-known poems reflect the theme of self-definition. Once we have discovered and learned to love ourselves, we will be in a better position to recognize the importance of sisterhood and the damage inflicted when we participate in what Lorde termed "horizontal hostility." Regarding self-love and acceptance Lorde (2007) states,

> nothing I accept about myself can be used against me to diminish me. I am who I am, doing what I came to do, acting upon you like a drug or chisel to remind you of your me-ness, as I discover you in myself. (147)

Discovering the power we hold within will only occur when we embrace the multiplicities of ourselves. When we deny, and alter these pieces, energy that could be used toward our creative missions is dissipated. We need to utilize our energy toward our personal liberation, recognizing any pieces of oppression we have swallowed and fighting to destroy that within us.

> With respect to myself specifically, I feel that not to be open about any of the different 'people'

within my identity, particularly the "mes" who are challenged by a status quo, is to invite myself and other women, by my example to live a lie. In other words, I would be giving in to a myth of sameness which I think can destroy us. (Lorde 2007, 118)

It is clear from the quote above that Lorde recognizes the multiplicities of self as an integral part of liberation.

Embracing ourselves will also allow us to conquer the fears that prevent us from embracing our sisters and brothers. In particular, Lorde writes extensively about the importance of sisterhood as a liberatory tool. Lack of sisterhood drains energy that could be used for our liberation. In addition, sisterhood forms a collective group, a shared wellspring (Evans 2007), which allows Black women to finally commune and lift each other to freedom. Lorde is not just concerned with a sisterhood between Black women, although she addresses this quite extensively throughout her poems. This is in response to the harsh outsider position she was often thrust into by her "sisters" because of her lesbianism, interracial marriage, unpermed hair, and so on. Lorde also writes about and recognized the interdependence of *all* women to reach freedom. She states "interdependency between women is the way to a freedom which allows I to be, not in order to be used, but in order to be creative" (Lorde 2007, 111).

Lorde's themes of survival through power, voice, adaptability, and self-love seamlessly intertwine to connect and overlap with each other providing a clear picture, for me, of my road to reclaiming my personal power. The next section explores the works of bell hooks as a vehicle for my professional liberation.

bell hooks: Transgressing as a Liberatory Practice

The epigraph by bell hooks (1994b) at the beginning of chapter 1 espouses the role of the African American educator throughout history. These educators, many of them Black females, realized the foundation of their "call" was built on liberatory practices. Many of them had to *transgress* in the name of progress. Yet at the same time, there has been an unyielding hunger and thirst for the "promise" of the future for those who have been, and continue to be, oppressed by institutional practices. bell hooks identifies this as the "yearning" coupled with a "cold awareness" of the presence of past oppressions. Readings and Schaber (1993) assert:

> For us, the postmodernism marks a gap in the thinking of time that is constitutive of the modernist concept of time as succession or progress. This is something we feel strongly about. It commits us here to resisting a number of existing images of the postmodern. We do not resist in the name of truth or purity, but in order to refuse that the postmodern be given a truth, circulated as current and legitimate coinage. (6)

This "spatial rift" or "split in time" can be connected to the "double consciousness" that was articulated by W. E. B. DuBois. The notion that African Americans, even as they have sought to build from within a full sense of authenticity, have had to exist in a nation where the fundamental symbolic structures continually place them in the position of the "other." As Ferguson (2000) argues:

> For African Americans, "race" as an identity and as a nexus of identification has never been theorized or experienced as a simple, unitary, decontextualized subject position. At the beginning of the twentieth century—long before the poststructuralist discovery of the socially invented, multiply positioned, nature of "self"— W. E. B. DuBois was describing the African American experience of self as unstable and dualistic. Blacks identified both as Americans, as "citizens," and as a racially subordinated minority that was excluded politically and socially. This "double consciousness," as he described it, has served as the matrix for identification as "Black" culturally and politically, grounding a culture of resistance and struggle against denial of the full rights of "citizens" because of "race." (205)

Gloria Jean

bell hooks (nee Gloria Jean Watkins) was born in 1952 in Hopkinsville, Kentucky, to a custodian father and homemaker mother. hooks's ontological viewpoint is based in part on a childhood fraught with patriarchy, domestic violence, and subordination. She attended segregated schools in rural Kentucky and struggled with belonging as a young child. With five sisters and one brother, hooks came from a house full of noise, but where ultimately she had no voice. This lack of a voice at home was part of the impetus for hooks dealing with her issues of subjectivity and voice throughout her career. Beginning at age nineteen, when she first published *Ain't I a Woman: Black Women and Feminism* (1981), she began a critical postmodern examination of race, class, and gender in the continued oppression of all peoples. As such, hooks is one of the premiere Black feminist writers to demand that people view these systems of oppression as interlocking.

Growing up, as I did, under the golden rule of "children should be seen and not heard," hooks wrote often of the importance of being "heard." Her writing is a form of psychological healing that affirms her existence, while informing others of the conditions of Black women in America. Her struggles with class and belonging speak to me and have motivated me to place her among the women to be analyzed for this book.

hooks brings several pieces to this book. I acknowledge her concept of choosing the margin as a space of radical openness. Utilizing the politics of location, hooks describes her view of transforming the margins in which Black women have been pushed into spaces that will "nourish one's capacity to resist...to imagine alternative, new worlds" (hooks 2004, 157). These spaces are important to Black women who may live and work at the center and are yet pushed to the margins daily. If we view the margins as only places of despair, we have the potential to embrace nihilism. For the purpose of this inquiry project, however, I focus more on how she utilizes the classroom, the academy, as one avenue to freedom.

Her main theme of liberation via educations is supported by language (privilege, class), freedom (self-love, belonging, fear, healing), teaching as a political act, and obedience (mind/body split). I selected hooks because I was looking for her to help me use "the margins as spaces of resistance." However, in reading her selected works, I came to see that she would help me most as a useful tool to discover, and rediscover, my passion for teaching. At the end of my formal educational journey, when most are excited to get into the academy, I am beginning to burnout. I saw it happening slowly; at first, it was less detail in my preparation for class. Next, I noticed that I became increasingly irritated with the students, for, well, being students. I know I was in danger, however, when I dreaded the drive to campus. I am not an expert on teaching and learning, but I do know this—if I don't have passion, I can't help ignite it in anyone else. This is why hooks's feelings of being "trapped" by the prospect of tenure, instead of excited, moved me so deeply. That's where and when we connected for this project. Her words would help me remember what education is about, a perfect complement to Lorde, who helped me rediscover what *I* am about.

There were several areas of connection between bell hooks and myself. We both felt displaced during our early school years; for hooks this was due to bussing, for me it was scholarships to attend private schools in the suburbs of Philadelphia. These feelings of displacement and isolation were exacerbated by our college experiences, in which we continued to be pressured to act as "native informants." I share with hooks an early sense of activism on campus as a way to push back, resist. She writes about the impact on her worldview of meeting Paulo Freire while she was an undergraduate student. Her passion for his ideas laid the theoretical framework for her remaining works. I had a similar pivotal moment as an undergraduate when I read *The Cress Theory of Color Confrontation and Racism* by Dr. Frances Cress Welsing (1970). Not only was I intrigued by her work, and the theoretical framework supporting it, but I continued to grow as I coordinated and hosted her visit to Penn State. Something about her presence, her spirit, gave me continued hope and renewed energy. Welsing embodied the following Thich Nhat Hanh statement:

> When you [the teacher] come and stay one hour with us, you bring that milieu...It is as though you bring a candle into the room. The candle is there, there is a kind of light-zone you bring in. When a sage is there and you sit near [her], you feel light, you feel peace. (as cited in hooks 1994b, 56)

I was drawn to Welsing as an image of the powerful Black woman I could become. I had choices, which did not involve begging to be let in to the patriarchal system of domination as a token. I had light, I felt peace.

hooks and I also share a need, as a result of this sense of displacement, to belong—to find a place that would feel like "home." She writes extensively about her search in her book *Belonging: A Culture of Place* (2008), and reading that work helped me understand that seeking out what one thinks is lost is normal—healthy, even. She states:

> Imagine then if you will, my childhood pain, I did not feel truly connected to these strange people, to these familial folks who could not only fail to grasp my worldview but who just simply did not want to hear it. As a child, I didn't know where I had come from. And when I was not desperately seeking to belong to this family community that never seemed to accept or want my, I was desperately trying to discover the place of my belonging. I was desperately trying to find my way home. (hooks 1994b, 60)

hooks's search for home also triggers another connection between us, not feeling included in the group we "belong" to (family) or with the "others," creating psychological tight spaces in which we must learn to navigate and manage our feelings and emotions in order to survive. hooks was an anomaly within her own home, with her very *family*. Throughout her work *Belonging*, she realizes that she cannot leave her past in the past, she must return to it and embrace it. She returns to Kentucky, "home," and continues her journey of healing and liberation. The realization happens for hooks, as it has for me, that she has always held the keys to her liberation inside of her.

Obedience

This desire to belong (with the "others") often goes along with obedience in the classroom. The theme of obedience really resonated with me. I instantly connected with her feelings of being an outsider as a result of being bused across rural Kentucky during desegregation. It was a result of being bused that she first begins to monitor herself and recognize that the goal of desegregation, stated as increasing diversity, really was about the illusion of difference. Our presence in those vanilla classrooms may have added a spot of color, but the atmosphere did not welcome our way of thinking or our cultural values. Instead "we were…showing how well we could become clones of our peers. As we constantly confronted biases, an undercurrent of stress diminished our learning experience" (hooks 1994b, 5). hooks reminds us that the environment is as important as the content in order for the learning process to fully occur. The expectation of "obedience" is counterintuitive to a natural environment of learning and growth and sets unrealistic expectations for students about education. As a result, educators truly interested in education as a practice of freedom will spend countless hours undoing the programming of many students, in order to unlock their true ability to learn—and, as a result, to be free.

The impact of demanding obedience in the classroom has real implications for all dimensions of our lives. If we believe, as hooks asserts, that teaching is a political act, then we are telling students that obedience and conformity, not education, is the way to freedom. hooks (1994b) states,

> if we examine critically the traditional role of the university in the pursuit of truth and the sharing of knowledge and information, it is painfully clear that biases that uphold and maintain white supremacy, imperialism, sexism and racism have distorted education so that is no longer about the practice of freedom. (29)

Teach us about "them"

An additional burden is placed on students who are asked to be the "native informant" for their group. This seemingly tempting position of insider is nothing more than the tokenism described earlier by Lorde as a way to lure someone in with the illusion that they will be either allowed to access some power or at the very least left alone. Being asked as a student to inform for or on one's group creates cognitive dissonance and is in direct contradiction to the liberation that occurs (according to Lorde) through sisterhood. Somewhere deep inside, the message that you will be allowed access in to the group is coupled with a hidden message that there is not room for everyone. Not only are we asked to act as "native informant"; but we begin to feel an unhealthy competition with those who can help provide our freedom—our brothers and sisters. We are *afraid*.

Mind/body split

To encourage obedience in the classroom, classrooms and universities have become places that reward students and teachers who live in the head but are not connected with their heart. This notion of universities as places for those smart in "book knowledge," reminds me of a saying from my grandmother "you're so smart, you're stupid." Never critically examining this statement, we thought she was just talking gibberish, underestimating her mother's wit...her Black mother inside. With more and acknowledged wisdom, I see this statement as profound. Those who disconnect their minds from their bodies lose a large part of themselves, and their ability to be free, by being void of feeling. Yet, to not conform in these new spaces could be an indication of membership in lower socioeconomic class and hurt ones chances to advance. hooks (1994b) states:

> As silence and obedience to authority were most rewarded, students learned that this was the appropriate demeanor in the classroom. Loudness, anger, emotional outbursts, and even something as seemingly innocent as unrestrained laughter were deemed unacceptable, vulgar disruptions of classroom social order. These

traits were also associated with being a member of the lower classes. If one was not from a privileged class group, adopting a demeanor similar to that of the group could help one to advance. (178)

Obedience is easier to enforce if you couple it with internal *fear* that those who are disobedient, already living on the edges of the social circle, will be labeled as "interlopers."

Where will *I* stand?

It was through reading hooks's book, *Where We Stand: Class Matters* (2000) that I, as an "interloper," first began to understand and expand my definition of class. Previously I had associated this term only as it correlated to income. The more money you made, the higher economic class you were in. Although this is accurate, I fell short of understanding "that class was more than just a question of money, that is shaped values, attitudes, social relations, and the biases that informed the way knowledge would be given and received" (hooks 2000, 178).

Struggling with issues surrounding class, and its resulting cultural capital (Delpit 1988), often place an additional burden on students who learn to balance their class locations. Students "must believe they can inhabit comfortably two different worlds, but they must make each space one of comfort. They must creatively invent ways to cross borders" (hooks 1994, 183)

Write it out—the power of and in language.

Creating spaces of comfort will demand an introspective healing process that addresses that *fear* that can accompany the discovery of the "true self." As both students and teachers we have to move away from internalized oppression that reinforces our participation in the patriarchal construction of education, and instead face our fears, address our feelings, and begin the process of healing. According to hooks (1994b), "to heal the splitting of the mind and body, we marginalized and oppressed people's attempt to recover ourselves and our experiences in language. We seek to make a place for intimacy" (175). Liberation through language as a healing property is an overlapping theme with Lorde. Finding ourselves, owning our power, will start with language and demand that we "make our words a counter-hegemonic speech liberating ourselves" (hooks 1994b, 175).

Language and disruption

hooks's view of language and the power it holds is twofold. First, she recognizes, as did Lorde, that language (in terms of reading and writing) holds healing properties and creates political statements. The spelling of hooks's name is a political statement. That seemingly small change, not capitalizing her first and last names, speaks volumes and creates discourses that impact the political, educational, and social landscapes, thereby creating spaces for change. hooks's refusal to capitalize her pen name is in an effort to ensure that people focus on the "substance of books, not who I am." This decision has created a discourse in classrooms, hallways, and blogs on the Internet. Is hooks breaking the rules? Why? One blogger was infuriated that hooks would not conform (read, "be obedient") in this respect.

She states, "If bell hooks thinks it's unimportant who writes a book, then why is she so determined that Black authors are quoted in discourse on postmodernism?" (DaLynziiChic 2006, para. 5). It is the author's humble opinion that the blogger has missed hooks's point. Too often people will read pieces by a particular author with a different, uncritical eye. This takes away from the content of the book and instead becomes a type of empty idol worship. hooks also makes a quiet stand by not placing "PhD" behind her name. Once again, some people are hesitant to critique a "doctor." Lorde shared this understanding of the power of language with hooks—not only in the vital necessity of poetry, but also in subtle ways.

Throughout *Sister Outsider*, I noticed small acts of resistance through language demonstrated by Lorde: in the phrase "women of Color" the *C* was always capitalized; "Black" women was always capitalized; "america" was not capitalized.

In *Discourse creates social change*, hooks (1994b) was right on target when she stated "like desire, language disrupts, refuses to be contained within boundaries" (167).

I ain't be got no weapon

The 1987 movie *Hollywood Shuffle* adopted a comedic approach to examining the role of Blacks in media. Through vignettes the actors mocked Blacksploitation films, creating a discourse (outside academia) regarding the role of Blacks in Hollywood. One common thread through all the vignettes was the use of Ebonics (also called Black English or Black Vernacular). Using Ebonics allowed Blacks to rally around a language that had been created out of need and was being used to heal.

Linguists have traced Ebonics back to slavery, when the need to communicate to the master and to each other demanded that slaves (from different tribes) quickly learn and use "broken English." Common language patterns were created (*out of isolation comes creation*), which were carried over for years, morphing into various dialects (Gullah) and reminding Blacks of our common starting place. Remnants of these dialectical differences can still be found today and have been studied and debated in academia (Dillard 1973; Smitherman 1977).

hooks also recognizes that language, Black vernacular, holds a unique space and fills a need for Black people in terms of liberation. The language created out of need to heal, to be free, holds a power that is negated when we are forced to adopt the language of our oppressor. Adrienne Rich notes in *The Burning of Paper Instead of Children*, "This is the oppressor's language yet I need it to talk to you" (as cited in hooks 1994b, 167). The contradiction inherent when a group is forced to learn the ways of another group to survive supports hooks assertion of the importance of using Black vernacular to claim our spaces. Black vernacular, now most often shared through rap music, has now been co-opted and/or discredited, leaving one standard by which all are measured. Ultimately, to coexist in both worlds, we are forced to learn the language of our oppressor. Even this personal exercise in liberation had to be constructed in the language of the oppressor. I am curious, then, of just how liberating this work will be given Lorde's assertion: "The master's tools will never dismantle the master's house."

The messages hooks tries to impart with her emphasis on language underscore her view of teaching as a political act. She states, "writing, I believed then, was all about private longing and personal glory, but teaching was about service, giving back to one's community. For Black folks, teaching—educating—was fundamentally political because it was rooted in antiracist struggle" (hooks 1994b, 2). This subtitle to *Teaching to Transgress* recognizes that freedom, liberation as an important goal that can be reached in the classroom, both as a teacher and as a student. A message I needed to hear at this stage of my professional journey, she states, "to have work that promotes one's liberation is such a powerful gift that it does not matter so much if the gift is flawed" (hooks 1994b, 50). Her view on the use of education as a tool for liberation is based on the premise that teaching is not just about the sharing of information with our students; it is also about sharing in their growth. This important message is often overlooked by the academy, as teaching is based on "rigor" and the competition that ensues among faculty is more about who is teaching the "harder" courses.

Give the people what they need.

As hooks heals herself through theorizing, writing, and teaching, she comes to understand that "any theory that cannot be shared in everyday conversation cannot be used to educate the public" (64). hooks (1994b) has been criticized for not producing work that is "scholarly" enough for the academy. She counters these attacks by stating,

> work by women of color and marginalized groups of white women (for example, lesbians, sex radicals) especially if written in a manner that renders it accessible to a broad reading public, is often de-legitimized in academic settings, even if the work enables and promotes feminist practice. (63–64)

This conundrum places Black women in academia in an interesting position. In order to receive tenure—and continue their political act of teaching—they must utilize "the oppressor's language" or find alternative venues of information sharing. I now fully understand why hooks panicked at the idea of receiving tenure. It is a life sentence.

Keeping information locked in the academy, through "top tier" journals, research symposiums, and conferences, may not be directly helpful to the masses and can be likened to an academic apartheid. A balance has to be struck between work that informs the academy and work that informs the soul. Sometimes there is overlap, oftentimes not. This debate will continue and is especially pertinent to this book as it relates to how discourse creates social change. bell hooks, despite the criticisms of scholarship, has created discourse that is useful in a variety of settings. Not only will you find her text used for classroom instruction, but you will also find it read in small groups at the coffee shop. This is what a discourse *must* be about.

My Afterthought

hooks's experiences provided her with opportunities for praxis, a chance to reflect on her work and connect it to action. The theme of liberatory praxis, which should be inherent in education, is supported by her understanding of the importance of language, self-love, the political act that is teaching, and obedience. hooks overlaps Lorde in many keys ways; but for my reading, it was more complementary, as they addressed different areas. For me to also practice what I am preaching, I must combine them into a useful template to propel me, and others in my situation, forward.

Embracing Sisterhood: A Meeting of the Minds

This experience has been overwhelming for me. It is like I have met, studied, and apprenticed with my sisters—Audre and bell. The spiritual connection we formed cannot be fully explicated on paper, nor should it be. I own it, it's mine, and selfishly there are pieces that I need for just me. With an overarching theme of survival for both Lorde and hooks, I have created subcategories of personal survival (Lorde) and professional survival (hooks) to anchor my reading. For Lorde survival came through a grand theme of power, which would be unleashed by discovering our voice (language, feelings), utilizing our adaptability, and recognizing self-love (self-definition, multiplicities of self, and sisterhood). For hooks it came through a grand theme of liberation via education supported by language (privilege, class), freedom (self-love, belonging, fear, healing), teaching as a political act, and obedience (mind/body split). Although their goal is the same, their approaches differ slightly.

Lorde earlier discussed how her life might have changed if she knew of Angelina Grimke while she was struggling at Hunter College. I guess I have to wonder what it might have been like for Lorde and hooks to interface: to tease out their ideas with each other and support each other through the journey. Lorde continues to do that for many people with her work. And that is the beauty of understanding what it means for you to survive and be free. Her work, her personal work, had a huge political impact and has allowed many women the opportunity to unlock their own doors toward freedom. I can only speculate if this is what she had in mind as she wrote, but my feelings from reading her work is that her primary goal was to free herself. Much like the well-known airplane advice—put your own oxygen mask on before attempting to help others.

Language

Lorde and hooks shared a commonality around the importance of language for liberation. hooks viewed language as an opportunity to disrupt the academy with simple political statements, such as noncapitalization of her name. She also recognized the organic nature of language that is created to heal. Her view of the importance of Black vernacular, or Ebonics, is a refreshing reminder to carefully examine all pieces of our cultural history before denouncing them as rooted in nothingness and, therefore, worthless. Lorde's approach to language was more directly tied to the therapeutic properties of poetry, journaling, and writing in general. It is through these actions, and (for her) specifically through poetry, that we will find—connect—to our Black poet, mother-wit, la facultad, which will allow us to reclaim our voice.

Fear

An undercurrent theme for both, fear is recognized as needing to be faced and conquered to move closer to freedom. Audre Lorde tackles fear in multiple ways across several of her poems and speeches.

For her, fear (being afraid) will stifle us and not allow us to connect to our feelings (Black poet inside!). This lack of connection will diminish our ability to work toward destroying the silences that render us voiceless.

hooks sees fear as connected to our need to practice self-love, become more confident in who we are and shed these pathological need to be "obedient" students. This will unlock a freedom within us that will connect body and mind *again*—like opening a valve— allowing us to freely flow back and forth within ourselves.

Self-love

> But the greatest of these is love
> —*1 Corinthians 13*

> You yourself, as much as anybody in the entire Universe, deserve your love and affection
> —*Buddha*

I have decided to start this section on self-love with two quotes that I live with daily. The first quote I have heard many times as a child in church. The second quote I discovered while in Portland, Oregon, and it struck right to my core. I dug around in my purse for paper and scribbled it down. I shared it as my quote on Facebook, not for the others, but for *me*, to remind *me* to love *me*. So I was struck by this theme from both women, and perhaps I was looking for it, but nonetheless, there it was. What I needed, when I needed it.

For hooks self-love comes with a sense of belonging, a discovery of the illusion of what we call "home," and a healing that allows us to be brave enough (no fear) to face ourselves and others. Lastly it demands that we learn to love and be loved. Lorde approached self-love from the perspective of embracing who we are (our many "me's"), and defining each part of us so that it will not be defined for us, and used against us. With this new ability to love ourselves comes the ability to reach out and build connections with our sisters so that we can support each other through this perilous journey.

Lorde's themes of personal survival via power continue to resonate with my soul. Her subthemes of voice, adaptability, and self-love provide several of the necessary tools I need in my toolbox of survival. The dialogue, an organic intellectual experience, allowed me to flush out several main themes and ideas through praxis. As I was writing the dialogue, I was practicing self-love, abolishing silence to reclaim my voice, and learning how to use my experiences to impact my future (adaptability).

Reading and recording hooks was accomplished in a different format, one more in line for the usefulness of her work to my project. As much as I personally owned Lorde's work, I could not address hooks in the same way. Professional survival is key to me, but my personal survival trumps all. With a slightly more clinical approach, I read hooks for the remaining keys that would help balance me out. Her theme of education as a tool for liberation kept me charged up not only to continue in my role as a professor in the academy but to complete and *embrace* this inquiry project. She saved me by illuminating this process. I am thankful. I recognized how I could make simple language changes and make a political act. My teaching is a political act. I challenged my obedience through her writing and could finally recognize how the pathological pieces of conformity were eating me alive. Her insistence on holistic education resonated with me and encouraged me to continue to attempt to connect with my students—mind and body—even though it may be physically and mentally exhausting. Finally, I recognized the need to examine her concepts of belonging and "home." These important pieces must be addressed and pushed through utilizing self-love and healing, the last few tools in my toolbox.

SIX

MY JOURNEY'S END

While on the path of completing this book, my goal was quite ambitious, at its best, and somewhat naïve. I realized when I began this project that several books could be written on Audre Lorde and bell hooks, and from multiple perspectives. Several books can and yet still will be written on these phenomenal Black feminist educators/scholars, as well as on the oppression of Black women in America.

Black Women Faculty and Historically Black Colleges and Universities

Black women historically have struggled for parity with White women and men in the American academy. They continue to be at the bottom of employment, rank, and tenure ladders at PWIs, and this pattern of gender inequity and discrimination is confounded by race at HBCUs. Scholars in the women's studies community have given some attention in recent years to the education of and climate for Black women at HBCUs. Guy-Sheftall's (1995) anthology of Black women's writing, *Words of Fire*, includes a few chapters describing the obstacles faced by Black women in the academy. Alexander's (1995) contribution to that work, though not specifically focused on the HBCU experience, details her mother's, her sister's, and her own struggles to obtain an education and utilize their professional training and skills. Hers is a discussion of financial hardship and lack of recognition due to gender and racial discrimination. She details, for example, the forces influencing her mother's decision to stay home and raise her three children instead of advancing her career in music. She also describes her sister's experiences of constant humiliation and harassment at the hands of male administrators while working at a small southern HBCU. That experience proved so difficult that her sister left the institution, vowing never to work at another Black school. Alexander later faced similar types of discrimination herself in her first job in academia, but at a PWI.

Wallace's (1995) contributed chapter in *Words of Fire* reflects upon the climate for Black women students at a particular HBCU campus in the 1960s. Recalling on her own undergraduate experiences there, Wallace notes that she left after her first semester because she found her female peers to be more focused on finding suitable mates than on advancing the collective status of Black people. She, on the other hand, was struggling to understand and reconcile what it meant to be a feminist. Her ideological conflicts in the

HBCU setting led to an overwhelming sense of isolation.

In her contribution to this debate, reprinted in *Words of Fire*, Beale (1995) described the phenomenon of double jeopardy, or dual exposure to racism and sexism, experienced by Black women at PWIs more than thirty years ago. Moses (1989) had earlier pursued this line of reasoning by examining the absence of Black women in the research literature on women in the academy. Her research explored the impact of the double obstacles of racism and sexism on Black women students and scholars. King (1988) also addressed the limitations of such dual-jeopardy models, pulling together a special issue of the feminist journal *Signs*, which argued that Black women face triple jeopardy instead—that is, the conflux of race, class, and gender discrimination and oppression—resulting from their unique sociohistorical circumstances.

Confounding the lack of leadership on campuses is the accompanying horizontal hostility (Lorde 2007) it creates. The personal and professional survival of Black women in academia, and in particular HBCUs, needs to be examined utilizing a different lens. Women of color and other marginalized groups are being shoved into models created for the rescue and support of White, heterosexual, able-bodied men. The unique atmosphere surrounding Black women at HBCUs demands further research and exploration. The survival strategies suggested for Black women at PWIs (discussed earlier in chapter 2) are not always applicable given the unique environment of the HBCU.

I suppose I naively thought that the common denominator of race would equalize, or at least soften, the playing field for Black women faculty at HBCUs. Instead, it appears as if patriarchy has become the order of the day. Within this oppositional framework of guarded binary thinking, I am wasting energy that can be used for campus change, personal growth, and liberation. The climate affects my ability to fully function, as energy I should be using in the pursuit of scholarly goals is oftentimes fretted away through basic psychic protection needs. This hypervigilance also leads to a decrease in physical health for many Black women. I often feel overwhelmed. We—*I*—desperately need more tools in our toolboxes to survive personally and professionally as Black women in academia.

"Survival Is Not an Academic Skill": Creating a Toolbox for Personal and Professional Survival

Having used my brain to navigate most of my life challenges, I thought I could do the same with my quest for survival in academe. I foolhardily subscribed to the mind and body split hooks refers to in many of her writings. As I now reflect on my efforts and the psychological aftermath, I realize that I could have tapped into my ancestral wellspring of coping mechanisms and skills. The quote at the beginning of this section is a wake-up call to all women of color, and other marginalized groups, trying to survive academia.

Without a clear roadmap of our own, Black women in academia (and particularly those at HBCUs) have continued doing what we have done for generations—be resilient.

Some of the coping methods I attempted to utilize were problematic in that they continue to portray me as "superwoman," assertive/aggressive, and indestructible. I started to buy into this myth and began to suffer from physical and mental anguish as a result. My colleagues and I continue to wander the hallways, tentatively reaching out to our female counterparts, afraid to ask for support and instead taking on additional tasks to prove their worth. The overlooked population of Black women at HBCUs has left a huge void in both research and practice and is worthy of further study. This book, largely designed to assist me in filling my personal toolbox, has potential usefulness for those in similar circumstances.

Breaking My Silence

Hill Collins (1998) supports the universal nature of the theme of "voice" found while reading the works of Lorde and hooks, calling it "breaking silence." Using this term, she discusses the importance of using literature as a counterhegemonic tool, which will begin a healing process both individually and collectively. Citing the works of Alice Walker, the Combahee River Collective, Toni Morrison, and Ntozake Shange, Hill Collins illustrates the power of literature for Black women in reclaiming their subjectivity via a variety of writing methods. According to Hill Collins (1998), when Black women break their silence individually (through autobiographies or books such as this), they/we are adding to and shifting the collective voice of Black women.

In particular Hill Collins (1998) discusses the importance of writing about "concrete experiences," stating that "when Black women valorize their own concrete experiences, they claim the authority of experience" (48). This authority disrupts other discourses that seek to subjugate marginalized groups by denying and/or overlooking the validity of lived experiences. This book was written utilizing my "authority of experience" in an attempt to disrupt other discourses and help me reclaim my voice. In doing so, this project recognizes the different worlds or "spheres" (Hill Collins 1998) in which Black women must learn to navigate.

Tools for Personal and Professional Survival

Documenting my lived experiences has proven to be an exercise in self-healing and liberation. The product of which has created more tools for my toolbox. These tools may be useful to others also traversing treacherous terrains, and I share with them this caveat: no one method can be used for all; however, Black women have created a standpoint that should allow for some commonalities for these tools. These tools are necessary in both the public and private spheres (Hill Collins 1998), and I acknowledge that although there may be a difference in spheres (public versus private); these tools connect seamlessly across multiple areas of our lives. If these tools are to be useful for survival, whether it is personal or professional, there must be an understanding that we cannot disconnect the various arenas of our lives. The fluidity of our existence and our self-preservation lies not in compartmentalizing areas but in learning to embrace the connectivity and overlaps that lie within and between.

The following tools may be helpful:

- Trust yourself—the Black poet/mother-wit/la facultad. Some call it intuition. Others might say "gut feeling." Whatever you name it, learn to be still enough to recognize that you are in touch with your personal truth. Whatever your spirit is whispers to you—acknowledge it and answer.

- Love yourself—as Buddha says, "you above all others deserve your love and affection." Self-love is paramount to our survival and our ability to thrive. This love needs to be holistic and encompass the many pieces of you. It may involve journaling, exercising, traveling, and daily affirmations. Loving yourself will also involve prioritizing your physical and mental needs. Recognize the subtle ways you may be sabotaging yourself with false narratives and negative "tapes." Challenge yourself. Is there not enough time to do the things you love to do, or are you not taking the time to do them?

- Develop a community—in both our personal and professional worlds, we all need support. Create a community that will assist you in moving toward your goals and dealing with the psychological tight spaces along the way. Be selective in your community building, as you must protect the energy you allow into your space. We all have a finite amount of energy, and if you allow energy drainers a regular seat at the table, there won't be enough you leftover for you. These communities can include "sistah-hoods" where you can learn to share your marginalization and resistance strategies. There will be healing properties that will come from those communal bonds.

- Mother yourself—as a Black female faculty member (especially at a HBCU), you will be expected to nurture many students along the way. In your personal life, as a mother and/or "other" mother, you will again be called upon for support. Mother yourself first.

- Discover your voice—the one deep down inside you, waiting to be heard. Let it out. Suppressing your voice will diminish your power, removing tools from your toolbox and placing them in the hands of your oppressors.

- Reconnect with your feelings—this will allow you to feel pleasure, pain, joy, and anger again. Being in touch with your feelings will allow you to fully experience life with every particle of your being.

- Re/discover the power of language—read the experiences of others and/or write your own. It is frustrating not having the language to articulate how you have been marginalized. Reading the scholarship related to your experiences will help you give voice to what's happening to you.

- Document your experiences—blogs, journals, or simple notes to yourself will allow you to track your experiences and monitor your growth. Most of all they will provide beginning tools for the generations following you.

- Engage in healthy living—you must experience wholeness. Wholeness is being in harmony with mind, body, and spirit. Commit to leading a holistically healthy life. Be mindful of how your mind and body connect, and be judicious regarding what elements you will allow into both.

Of course these suggestions are merely that—suggestions. However, they can begin to fill your toolbox. You will identify and utilize additional ones to include, and you may remove a tool here and there. The process of healing and survival is fluid and individual. Allow it to happen and embrace it.

Additional research is needed on the psychological impact of negotiating the unique atmosphere and challenges HBCUs present—to progress the souls, hearts, and minds of students while creating antioppressive environments for women of color, particularly Black women. As there is no monolithic experience, there is also no one key that will unlock every door. However, the more keys in our possession, the greater our chances of opening the door to our liberation.

My hope is that this book will provide one key for future use.

REFERENCES

Aggers, B. (1992). *Cultural studies as critical theory.*
London: Falmer Press.

Aigner-Varoz, E. (2000). Metaphors of a Mestiza
Consciousness: Anzaldua's Borderlands/La
Frontera. *Melus, 25,* 47-62.

Alexander, M. W. (1995). Black women in academia.
In B. Guy-Sheftall (Ed.). *Words of fire: An
anthology of african-american feminist thought* (pp. 454-
460). New York: The New Press.

Alexander, M. & Mohanty, C. (1997). *Feminist
genealogies, colonial legacies, democratic futures.* New
York: Routledge.

Alexander-Floyd, N. G., & Simien, E. M. (2006).
Revisiting "What's in a name?": Exploring the
contours of africana womanist thought. *Frontiers,*
67-89.

Alkalimat, A. (1986). *Introduction to afro-american studies: A people's college primer.* Chicago: Twenty-First Century Books.

Anderson, T. (1988). Black encounter of racism and elitism in white academe: a critique of the system. *Journal of Black Studies,* 259-272.

Anzaldua, G. (1987). *Borderlands la frontera: The new mestiza.* San Francisco: Aunt Lute.

Appleby, G. A., Colon, E., & Hamilton, J. (2001). *Diversity, oppression and functioning: Person-in environment assessment and intervention.* Boston: Allyn & Bacon.

Arango, S. (1993). *African American women on predominantly white campuses.* (Unpublished Master's Thesis). The Pennsylvania State University Graduate School; Counselor Education Program.

Austin, R. (1989). Sapphire Bound! *Wisconsin Law Review,* 539.

Bambara, T. C. (1970). *The black woman: An anthology.* New York: Washington Square.

Beale, F. M. (1969). *Black women's manifesto; Double jeopardy: To be black and female. In Third World*

Women's Alliance, Black Women's Manifesto (n.d.). New York: Third World Women's Alliance.

Beale, F. M. (1995). Double jeapordy: To be black and female. In B. Guy-Sheftall (Ed.). *Words of fire: An anthology of african-american feminist thought* (pp. 146-156). New York: The New Press.

Beckham, B. (1988). Strangers in a strange land: The experience of blacks on white campuses. *Educational Record*, 74-78.

Belenky, M. F., Clinchy, B. M., Goldberger, N. R., & Tarule, J. M. (1986). *Women's ways of knowing*. New York: Bantam Books.

Bell, E. L. (1990). The bicultural life experience of career-oriented black women. *Journal of Organization Behavior*, 459-477.

Bennett Jr., L. (1988). *Before the Mayflower: A history of black America*. New York: Penguin.

Beoku-Batts, J., & Njambi, W. N. (2009) African feminist scholars in women's studies: Negotiating spaces of dislocation and transformation in the study of women. In S. Foster, F. S. Foster, & B. Guy-Sheftall (Eds.), *Still brave: The evolution of black women's studies* (pp. 300-317). New York: Feminist Press.

Berger, M. T., & Guidroz, K. (2009). *The intersectional approach: Transforming the academy through race, class, & gender*. Chapel Hill: The University of North Carolina Press.

Billingslea-Brown, A.J., & Gonzalez de Allen, G. J. (2009). Discourses of diversity at spelman college. In W. R. Brown-Glaude (Ed.), *Doing Diversity in Higher Education* (pp. 39-60). Piscataway: Rutgers University Press.

Birnbaum, N. (1971). *Toward a critical sociology*. Oxford: Oxford University Press.

Bonilla-Silva, E. (2006). *Racism with racists: Color-blind racism and the persistence of racial inequality in the United States*. Lanham, MD: Rowman & Littlefield.

Bottomore, T. (1984). *The Frankfurt School*. London: Tavistock.

Boyd, W. (1973). Black student, white college. *College Board Review*, 18-25.

Brock, R. (2005). *Sista talk: The personal and the pedagogical*. New York: Peter Lang.

Burke, B., Cropper, A., & Harrison, P. (2000). Real or imagined—Black women's experiences in the academy. *Community, Work & Family*, 297-310.

Burrell, L. F. (1980). Is there a future for black students on predominantly white campuses? *Integrateducation*, 23-27.

Burrow, Jr., R. (1994). James H. Cone and black liberation theology. Jefferson: McFarland & Company.

Bush, V. B., Chambers, C. R., & Walpole, M. (2009). *From diplomas to doctorates: The success of black women in higher education and its implications for equal opportunities for all*. Sterling: Stylus.

Butler, J. (1988). Performative acts and gender constitution: An essay in phenomenology and feminist theory. *Theatre Journal*, 519-531.

Butler, J. (2007). *Gender trouble*. New York: Routledge.

Byrd, R., Betsch-Cole, J., & Guy-Sheftall, B. (2009). *I am your sister: Collected and unpublished writings of Audre Lorde*. New York: Oxford University Press.

Brown-Glaude, W. R. (2010). But some of us are brave: Black women faculty transforming the academy. *Signs: Journal of Women in Culture and Society*, 801-809.

Byrne-Armstrong, H., Higgs, J., & Horsfall, D. E. (2001). Critical moments in qualitative research. Woburn: Buttersworth-Heinemann.

Calhoun, C. J. (1995). *Critical social theory: Culture, history, and the challenge of difference.* Cambridge: Blackwell.

Camp, S. M. (2004). *Closer to freedom.* Chapel Hill: The University of North Carolina Press.

Carroll, C. (1982). Three's a crowd: The dilemma of the black woman in higher education. In G. Hull, P. Bell Scott, & B. Smith (Eds.), *But some of us are brave* (pp. 117-128). New York: Feminist Press.

Carter-Black, J. (2008). A black woman's journey into a predominantly white academic world. *Journal of Women and Social Work*, 112-122.

Combahee River Collective. (1983). A Black feminist statement. In C. Moraga & G. Anzaldua (Eds.), *This bridge called my back: Writings by radical women of color* (pp. 210-218). New York: Kitchen Table Women of Color Press.

Cone, J. H. (1970). *A black theology of liberation.* Philadelphia: J. B. Lippincott Company.

Contreras, A. R. (1998). Leading from the margins in the ivory tower. In L. A. Valverde & L. A. Castenell, L. A. (Eds.), Strategies for transforming higher education. Walnut Creek: AltiMira Press.

Cooper, C. W., & Gause, C. P. (2007). Who's afraid of the big bad wolf? Facing identity politics and resistance when teaching for social justice. In D. Carlson & C. P. Gause (Eds.), *Keeping the promise: Essays on leadership, democracy and education* (pp. 197-216). New York: Peter Lang.

Coulthard, M. (1985). *An introduction to discourse analysis.* Harlow: Pearson Education Limited.

Crenshaw, K. G., Gotanda, N., Peller, G., & Thomas, K. (1995). *Critical race theory: The key writings that formed the movement.* New York: The New Press.

DaLynziiChic. (2006, September 13). Why bell hooks doesn't capitalize her name, and why this makes her argument moot [Web log message]. Retrieved from http://machines.pomona.edu/190-2006/node/65.

Daly, A., Jennings, J., Beckett, J. O., & Leashore, B. R. (1995). Effective coping strategies of African Americans. *Social Work, 40*(2), 240-248.

Davis, A. (1983). *Women, race, & class*. New York: First Vintage Books.

Davis, A. (1994). Black women in the academy. *Callaloo*, 422-431.

DeCuir-Gunby, J.T., Long-Mitchell, L.A., & Grant, C. (2009). The emotionality of women professors of color in engineering: A critical race theory and critical race feminism perspective. In P. Schutz & M. Zembylas (Eds.), *Advances in teacher emotion research: The impact on teachers' lives* (pp. 323-342). New York: Springer.

Delpit, L. (1988). The silenced dialogue: Power and pedagogy in educating other people's children. *Harvard Educational Review, 58*(3), 280-298.

Denzin, N., & Lincoln, Y. (1994). *Handbook of qualitative research*. Thousand Oaks, CA: Sage.

Denzin, N., & Lincoln, Y. (2003). Collecting and interpreting qualitative materials (2nd ed.). Thousand Oaks, CA: Sage.

Dillard, J. L. (1973). *Black english*. New York: Random House.

Dinka, F., Mazzella, F., & Pilany, D. (1980). Reconciliation and confirmation: Blacks and whites at a predominantly white university. *Journal of Black Studies*, 55-76.

DuBois, W. E. B. (1990). *The souls of black folk*. New York: Vintage.

Early, G. (1993). Lure and loathing: Essays on race, identity, and the ambivalence of assimilation. New York: Penguin.

Ellison, R. (1989). *Invisible man*. New York: Vintage Books.

Erikson, E. H. (1968). *Identity: Youth and crisis*. New York: Norton & Company.

Essed, P. (1991). *Understanding everyday racism: An interdisciplinary theory*. Newbury Park: Sage.

Evans, S. Y. (2007). *Black women in the ivory tower, 1850-1954: An intellectual history*. Gainesville, FL: University Press of Florida.

Fairclough, N. (2003). *Analysing discourse*. London: Routledge.

Fairclough, N. (1995). *Critical discourse analysis: The critical study of language.* New York: Longman Group.

Fairclough, N., & Chouliaraki, L. (1999). *Discourse in late modernity.* Edinburgh: Edinburgh University Press.

Fairclough, N.& Wodak, R. (1997) Critical discourse analysis. In: T. Van Dijk (Hg.): Discourse Studies: A Multidisciplinary Introduction. Vol. 2. London: Sage, s. 258-84.

Fanon, F. (1967). *Black skins, white masks.* New York: Grove Press.

Feagin, J. R., & Sikes, M. P. (1994). *Living with racism: The black middle-class experience.* Boston: Beacon Press.

Ferguson, R. (2000). The nightmares of the heteronormative. *Cultural Values*, 419-444.

Fleming, J. (1984). *Blacks in college.* San Francisco: Jossey-Bass.

Foucault, M. (1979). *Discipline and punish: Birth of a prison.* New York: Vintage Books.

Franklin, J. H., & Moss Jr., A. A. (1994). From slavery to freedom: A history of African Americans. New York: McGraw-Hill.

Friedan, B. (1963). *The feminine mystique*. New York: W. W. Norton.

Gaspar, D. B., & Hine, D. C. (1996). More than chattel: Black women and slavery in the Americas. Bloomington, IN: Indiana University Press.

Gates Jr., H. L., & McKay, N. Y. (1997). The Norton Anthology of African American literature. New York: W. W. Norton & Company, Inc.

Gause, C. P. (2001). *How African-American educators "make sense" of hip hop culture and its influence on public schools: A case study*. Unpublished doctoral book. Miami, OH: Miami University.

Gause, C. P. (2008). *Integration matters*. New York: Peter Lang.

Giddings, P. (1984). *When and where I enter: The impact of black women on race and sex in America*. New York: Bantam.

Gillespie, R. R. C. (2009). Is the leadership in the black church complicit in the perpetuation of dominance and oppression? (Unpublished doctoral book). University of North Carolina at Greensboro, Greensboro.

Gilligan, C. (1982). *In a different voice: Psychological theory and women's development.* Cambridge: Harvard University Press.

Glass, K. L. (2005). Tending to the roots: Anna Julia Cooper's sociopolitical thought and activism. *Meridians: Feminism, Race, Transnationalism,* 23-55.

Glesne, C. (2006). *Becoming qualitative researchers: An introduction* (3rd ed.). Boston: Pearson.

Goodall Jr., H. (2000). *Writing the new ethnography.* Lanham: Rowman & Littlefield.

Gordon, D. B. (2003). Rhetoric, ideology, and nineteenth-century black nationalism. Carbondale, IL: Southern Illinois University Press.

Gregory, S. T. (1995). *Black women in the academy: The secrets to success and achievement.* Latham: University Press of America.

Gregory, S. T. (2001). Black faculty women in the academy: History, status, and future. *Journal of Negro Education,* 124-136.

Guy-Sheftall, B. (Ed.). (1995). *Words of fire: An anthology of African-American feminist thought.* New York: The New Press.

Hall, R. E. (2006). White women as a postmodern vehicle of black oppression: The pedagogy of discrimination in western academe. *Journal of Black Studies*, 69-82.

Hammond, K. (1980). An interview with Audre Lorde. *American Poetry Review*, 18-21.

Hammond, K. (1981). Audre Lorde: Interview. *Denver quarterly*, 10-27.

Harding, S. (2004). *The feminist standpoint reader: Intellectual and political controversies.* New York: Routledge.

Harley, D. A. (2008). Maids of academe: African American women faculty at predominantly white institutions. *Journal of African American Studies*, 19-36.

Harrison, R. K. (2009). *Enslaved women and the art of resistance in antebellum America.* New York: Palgrave Macmillan.

Hatch, J. (2002). *Doing qualitative research in education settings.* Albany: State University of New York Press.

Helms, J. (1990). *Black and white racial identity: Theory, research, and practice.* New York: Greenwood.

Hesse-Biber, S. N., & Leavy, P. L. (2006). *The practice of qualitative research.* Thousand Oaks, CA: Sage.

Hesse-Biber, S. N., & Leavy, P. L. (2007). *Feminist research practice.* London: Sage.

Hill Collins, P. (1990). *Black feminist thought: Knowledge, consciousness, and the politics of empowerment.* New York: Routledge.

Hill Collins, P. (2003). Toward an afrocentric feminist epistemology. In Y. S. Lincoln & N. K. Denzin (Eds.), Turning points in qualitative research: Tying knots in a handkerchief. Walnut Creek: AltaMira.

Hill Collins, P. (1998). *Fighting words: Black women and the search for justice.* Minneapolis, MN: University of Minneapolis Press.

Hill Collins, P. (2009). *Black feminist thought: Knowledge, consciousness, and the politics of empowerment* (2nd ed.). New York: Routledge.

Hill, D. K. (2009). Code-switching pedagogies and African American student voices: Acceptance and resistance. *Journal of Adolescent & Adult Literacy*, 120-131.

Hinton, K. (2004). "Sturdy black bridges": Discussing race, class, and gender. *The English Journal*, 60-64.

Holt, T. (1995). Afterword: Mapping the black public sphere. In The Black Public Sphere Collective (Eds.), *The black public sphere: A public culture book* (pp. 325-328). Chicago: The University of Chicago Press.

hooks, b. (1981). *Ain't I a woman: Black women and feminism*. Boston: South End.

hooks, b. (1989). *Thinking feminist, thinking black*. Boston: South End Press.

hooks, b. (1990). *Yearning: Race, gender, and cultural politics*. Boston: South End Press.

hooks, b. (1993). *Sisters of the yam: Black women and self-recovery*. Boston: South End.

hooks, b. (1994b). Teaching to transgress: Education as the practice of freedom. New York: Routledge.

hooks, b. (1995). *Killing rage: Ending racism.* New York: Holt.

hooks, b. (1996). Sisterhood: Beyond public and private. *Signs: Journal of Women in Culture and Society,* 814-829.

hooks, b. (2000). *Where we stand: Class matters.* New York: Routledge.

hooks, b. (2004). *Feminist theory: From margin to center.* Cambridge: South End Press.

hooks, b. (2008). *Belonging: A culture of place.* New York: Routledge.

hooks, b., & West, C. (1991). *Breaking bread: Insurgent black intellectual life.* Boston: South End.

Horrocks, C., & Jevtic, Z. (2002). *Introducing Foucault.* Thriplow: Icon Books.

Howard-Vital, M. (1989). African American women in higher education: Struggling to gain identity. *Journal of Black Studies,* 180-191.

Hudson-Weems, C. (1989). Cultural and agenda conflicts in academia: Critical issues for Africana women's studies. *Western Journal of Black Studies, 13*(4), 185-189.

Hughes, M. (1987). Black students participation in higher education. *Journal of College Student Personnel*, 532-545.

Hytten, K. (2004). Postcritical ethnography: Research as a pedagogical encounter. In G. Noblit, S. Flores, & E. Hurillo (Eds.), *Postcritical ethnography: Reinscribing critique* (pp. 95-105). Crosskill: Hampton Press.

Ihle, E. L. (1992). *Black women in higher education: An anthology of essays, studies and documents*. New York: Garland.

Jacobs, H. (2001). Incidents in the life of a slave girl. Mineola: Dover Publications, Inc.

Jones, C., & Shorter-Gooden, K. (2003). Shifting: The double lives of black women in America. New York: Harper.

Jones, J. (1985). *Labor of love, labor of sorrow*. New York: Vintage Books.

Jung, C. G. (1964). *Man and his symbols*. London: Aldus Books.

Jung, C. G. (1991). Psychology of the unconscious. Princeton: Princeton University Press.

Kanter, R. M. (1977). Men and Women of the Corporation. New York: BasicBooks.

Kelly, H. (2007). Racial tokenism in the school workplace: An exploratory study of black teachers in overwhelmingly white schools. *Educational Studies: Journal of the American Educational Studies Association*, 230-254.

King, D. K. (1988). Multiple jeopardy, multiple consciousness: The context of a black feminist ideology. *Signs*, 42-72.

Kleinbaum, D., & Kleinbaum, A. (1976). The minority experience at a predominantly white university—A report of a 1972 survey at the University of North Carolina at Chapel Hill. *Journal of Negro Education*, 312-328.

Kolchin, P. (1993). *American slavery: 1619-1877*. New York: Hill and Wang.

Landrine, H., & Klonoff, E. (1996). African American acculturation: Deconstructing race and reviving culture. San Francisco: Sage.

Leary, M. R., & Tangney, J. P. (2003). *Handbook of self and identity*. New York: Guildford Press.

Lerner, G. (1972). *Black women in white America: A documentary history.* New York: Vintage.

Lincoln, Y. S., & Denzin, N. K. (2003). *Turning points in qualitative research: Tying knots in a handkerchief.* Walnut Creek, CA: AltaMira.

Lincoln, Y. S., & Guba, E. G. (1985). *Naturalistic inquiry.* Thousand Oaks, CA: Sage.

Lorde, A. (1978). *The black unicorn.* New York: W. W. Norton & Company.

Lorde, A. (1982). *Zami: A new spelling of my name.* Freedom: Crossing Press.

Lorde, A. (2007). *Sister outsider.* Berkeley: Crossing Press.

Luke, A. (1977). Critical approaches to literacy. In Edwards and Corson (Eds.), *Encyclopedia of language and education,* (pp. 143-152). Dordrecht: Kluwer Academic Publishers.

Madison, D. S. (2005). *Critical ethnography: Methods, ethics, and performance.* New York: Sage.

McAdoo, H. (1997). *Black families.* San Francisco: Sage.

McCann, C. R., & Kim, S. (2003). *Feminist theory reader: Local and global perspectives.* New York: Taylor & Francis.

Merriam, S.B. (1988). *Qualitative research and case study applications in education.* San Francisco: Jossey-Bass.

Mey, J. (1985). *Whose language: A study in linguistic pragmatics.* Amsterdam: John Benjamins Publishing.

Mills, S. (2003). *Michel Foucault.* New York: Routledge.

Morgan, J. L. (2004). *Laboring women: Reproduction and gender in the new world slavery.* Philadelphia: University of Pennsylvania Press.

Moses, Y. T. (1989). *Black women in academe: Issues and strategies.* Washington: Association of American Colleges.

Nelson, L.W. (1990). Code-switching in the oral life of narratives of African-American women: Challenges to linguistic hegemony. *Journal of Education,* 142-155.

Noddings, N. (1984). *Caring: A feminine approach to ethics & moral education.* Berkeley: University of California Press.

Owens Moore, T. (2005). A fanonian perspective on double consciousness. *Journal of Black Studies*, 751-762.

Padillo, A. (1984). Ethnic minority scholars, researchers, and mentoring: Current and future issues. *Educational Researcher*, 24-27.

Patton, M. (1980). *Qualitative evaluation methods*. Thousand Oaks, CA: Sage Publications.

Patton, M. (2002). *Qualitative research & evaluation methods*. Thousand Oaks, CA: Sage Publications.

Perkins, L. (1983). The impact of the "cult of true womanhood" on the education of black women. *Journal of Social Issues*, 17-28.

Pifer, A. (1973). The higher education of blacks in the United States. *South African Institute on Race Relations*, 1-52.

Radford-Hill, S. (2000). *Further to fly: Black women and the politics of empowerment*. Minneapolis, MN: University of Minnesota Press.

Rainbow, P. (1984). *The Foucault reader*. New York: Pantheon Books.

Rasmussen, D. M. (Ed.). (1996). *The handbook of critical theory*. Oxford: Blackwell Publishers.

Readings, B., & Schaber, B. (Eds.). (1993). *Postmodernism across the ages*. Syracuse, NY: Syracuse University Press.

Robbins, B. (1993). *The phantom public sphere*. Minneapolis, MN: University of Minnesota Press.

Roseboro, D., & Gause, C. P. (2009). Faculty of color constructing communities at predominantly white institutions. In C. A. Mullen (Ed.), *Leadership and building professional learning communities* (pp. 139-150). New York: Palgrave Macmillan.

Roth, B. (2004). *Separate roads to feminism: Black, chicana, and white feminists movements in Atmerica's second wave*. Cambridge: Cambridge University Press.

Schneck, S. F. (1987). Michael Foucault on power/discourse, theory and practice. *Human Studies*, 15-33.

Shorter-Gooden, K. (2004). Multiple resistance strategies: How African American women cope with racism and sexism. *Journal of Black Psychology*, 406-425.

Silverman, D. (2006). *Interpreting qualitative data.*
London: Sage.

Smart, B. (1993). *Postmodernity.* London: Routledge.

Smart, B. (2002). *Michel Foucault: Revised edition.*
London: Routledge.

Smitherman, G. (1977). *Talkin and testifyin: The language
of black Americans.* Detroit: Houghton Mifflin
Company.

Springer, K. (2002). Third wave black feminism?
Signs: Journal of Women in Culture and Society, 1059-
1082.

St. Jean, Y., & Feagin, J. R. (1998). Double burden:
Black women and everyday racism. Armonk: M.
E. Sharpe.

Sterling, D. (1984). *We are your sisters: Black women in
the nineteenth century.* New York: W. W. Norton
Company.

Takaki, R. (1993). *A different mirror: A history of
multicultural America.* Boston: Little, Brown and
Company.

Tatum, B. D. (1987). *Assimilation blues: Black families in white communities, who succeeds and why?* New York: Greenwood Press.

Tatum, D. J., & McEwen, M. K. (1992). The relationship of racial identity attitudes to autonomy and mature interpersonal relationships in black and white undergraduate women. *Journal of College Student Personnel,* 439-446.

Terhune, C. P. (2007). Coping in isolation: The experiences of black women in white communities. *Journal of Black Studies,* 547-564.

Thomas, G. D., & Hollenshead, C. (2001). Resisting from the margins: Coping strategies of black women and other women of color faculty members at a research university. *Journal of Negro Education,* 166-175.

Thompson, M. (2002). ICT, power, and development discourse: A critical analysis. *The Electronic Journal of Information Systems in Developing Countries, 20*(4), 1-26.

Turner, C. S. (2002). Women of color in academe: Living with multiple marginality. *The Journal of Higher Education,* 74-93.

Van Leeuwen, T. (2008). *Discourse and practice: New tools for critical discourse analysis.* New York: Oxford University Press.

Villaverde, L. E. (2008). *Feminist theories and education.* New York: Peter Lang.

Walker, A. (1983). *In search of our mothers' gardens.* Orlando: Harcourt Bruce Jonavich.

Wallace, M. (1983). *Black popular culture.* New York: The New Press.

Wallace, M. (1995). Anger in isolation: A black feminist's search for sisterhood. In B. Guy-Sheftall (Ed.). *Words of fire: An anthology of african-american feminist thought* (pp. 220-228). New York: The New Press.

Wallace, M. (2004). *Dark designs & visual culture.* Durham: Duke University Press.

Weisbrot, R. (1991). Freedom bound: A history of America's civil rights movement. New York: Penguin.

Welsing, F. C. (1970). *The Cress Theory of Color Confrontation and Racism (white supremacy).* Washington: C-R Publishers.

West, C. (1993). *Race matters*. Boston: Beacon Press.

West, C. (1999). *The Cornel West reader*. New York: Basic Civitas Book.

White, D. G. (2008). *Telling histories: Black women historians in the ivory tower*. Chapel Hill: The University of North Carolina Press.

Willie, C. V., & McCord, A. S. (1972). *Black students at white colleges*. New York: Praeger.

Wills, J. W. (2007). Foundations of qualitative research: Interpretive and critical approaches. Thousand Oaks, CA: Sage.

Wilson, B., & Miller, R. (2002). Strategies for managing heterosexism among African American gay and bisexual men. *Journal of Black Psychology*, 371-391.

Wilson, H. (2009). *Our nig: Sketches from the life of a free black*. Lexington: Seven Treasures Publications.

Wing, A. K. (1997). *Critical race feminism: A reader*. New York: New York University Press.

Wodak, R., & Chilton, P. (2005). *A new agenda in (critical) discourse analysis*. Amsterdam: John Benjamins.

Wodak, R., & Meyer, M. (Eds.). (2009). *Methods of Critical Discourse Analysis*. London: Sage.

Wood, L. A., & Kroger, R. O. (2000). *Doing discourse analysis: Methods for studying action in talk and text*. Thousand Oaks, CA: Sage.

Made in the USA
San Bernardino, CA
31 December 2015